Music Theory for Singers

Level Five

Second Edition

Sarah Sandvig

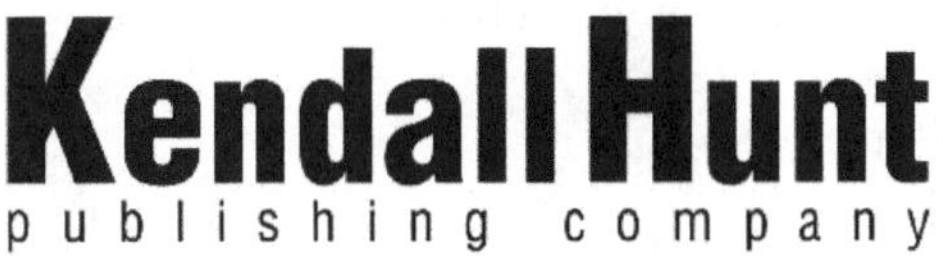

Cover image © Shutterstock, Inc. Used under license.
Back cover image and all keyboard images provided
by the author.

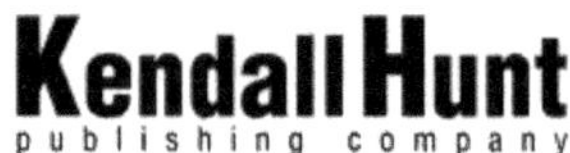

www.kendallhunt.com
Send all inquiries to:
4050 Westmark Drive
Dubuque, IA 52004-1840

ISBN 978-1-5249-1440-0

Published in the United States of America

FOREWORD

In Sarah Sandvig's *Music Theory for Singers*, voice students and their teachers finally have a singer-friendly primer for musicianship and music theory that is directly applicable to voice training. Mrs. Sandvig has capitalized on her experience as a successful private voice teacher to create this comprehensive workbook, which, in clear, concise language, lays out an easy-to-follow lesson plan progressing from basic through advanced skills. *Music Theory for Singers* is equally applicable in a college or high school classroom setting as in the private studio, and voice teachers will especially appreciate the inclusion of international musical terminology, and music history which their students are likely to encounter in vocal repertoire. For teens studying voice for the first time, as well as for life-long adult singers, *Music Theory for Singers* will become a valued adjunct to any level of vocal study.

Juliana Gondek
Metropolitan Opera soloist and
Prize-winning international recording artist
Professor and Chair, Division of Voice Studies
UCLA

I am beginning my first semester as a BFA Musical Theatre Major at The Boston Conservatory at Berklee. I used Sarah's theory books throughout high school from levels 5 through 10, and they have prepared me immensely for this first semester – and beyond. For example, I recently went through a music theory and sight singing placement test: I was so amazed how comfortable I felt with both the written and singing portions. It was everything I had already learned from these theory books – key signatures, scales, rhythm, solfege, and more. In addition, I became so familiar with the fundamentals of music and a piano keyboard (even through utilizing the vocal theory books) I was able to test out of a whole year of beginner piano. All of this creates the possibility for me to move on to higher levels and be more challenged than if I had to start from the basics. Not to mention all of the composers and terms that are necessary knowledge to be successful in professional music classes and settings. It feels good to know that if I am ever unsure about what I am learning in class, my theory books are right there on the bookshelf to help me out.

Sofia Ross
Musical Theatre Major
Boston Conservatory

Thank you to the following people for their help and guidance in writing these books: Mary Beard, Melissa Caldretti, Sally Curry, Sharlae Jenkins, Vanessa Parvin, Connie Venti & my dad, Ken Watson.

Thank you to my husband Darren and sons Aiden & Caleb for their love, support and patience throughout this writing process.

NOTE TO TEACHER:
These books are a supplement to private, group or classroom voice lessons, and though I feel they can stand alone, they are not meant as a replacement for a good teacher who ensures student learning and understanding of music theory, history, and sight-singing. Each book includes reviews of subjects with a review test (with answers) at the end. You may also purchase the Answer Key, which has answers to all pages in each level, 1-10. Composers, terms, IPA and solfege are unique elements of these books that make them especially helpful for singers.

I hope these books are a useful addition to the many tools you already utilize to teach young singers in your studio or classroom.

TABLE OF CONTENTS

MUSIC THEORY FOR SINGERS

LEVEL 5

Review of Concepts in Level 4

Half Steps and Whole Steps

A half step is the distance between one pitch and the very next pitch, higher or lower.
A whole step is the same as two half steps.

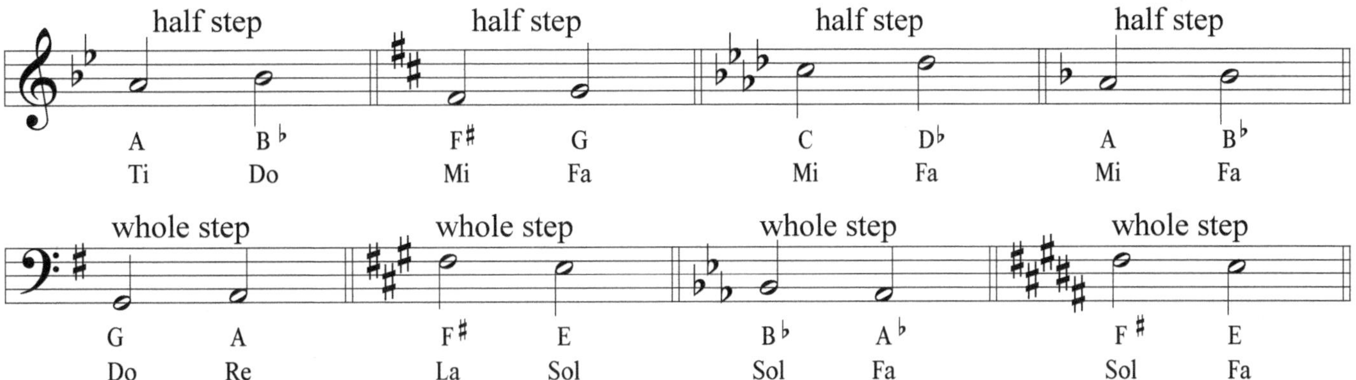

Notes, Rhythm & Time Signature: Review

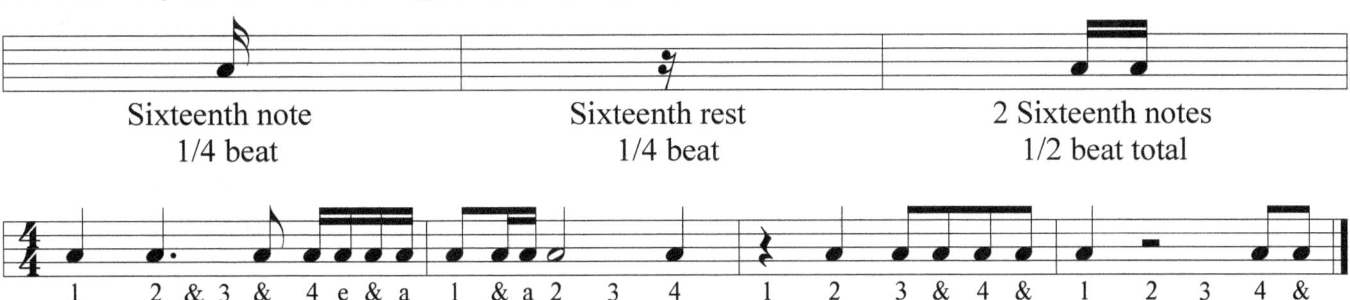

Key Signature & Triad Review

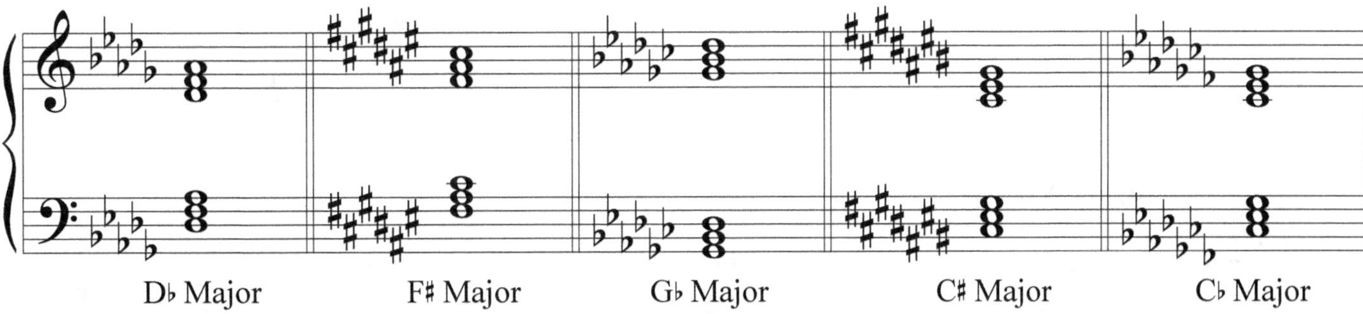

Interval Review

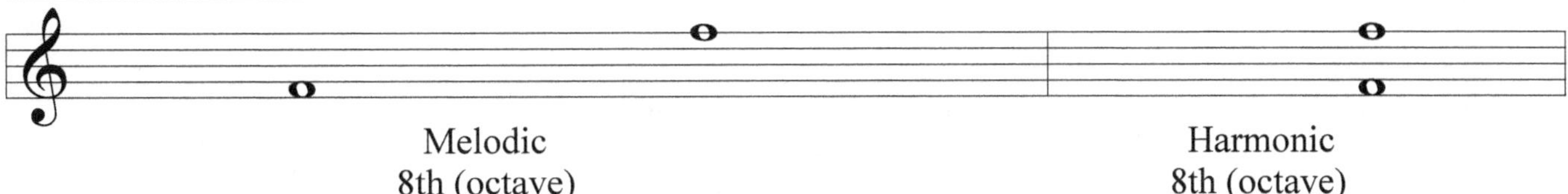

Order of Sharps & Flats

♯ - The order of sharps in a key signature is: F, C, G, D, A, E, B. You can use the following saying to remember the order of the sharps: (**F**at **C**ats **G**o **D**own **A**lleys **E**ating **B**urritos)

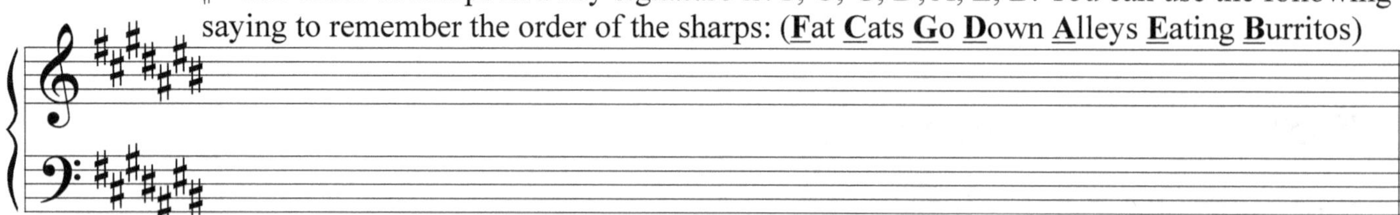

♭ - The order of flats in a key signature is: B, E, A, D, G, C, F. You can use the following saying to remember the order of the flats: (**BEAD** - **G**um **C**andy **F**ruit)

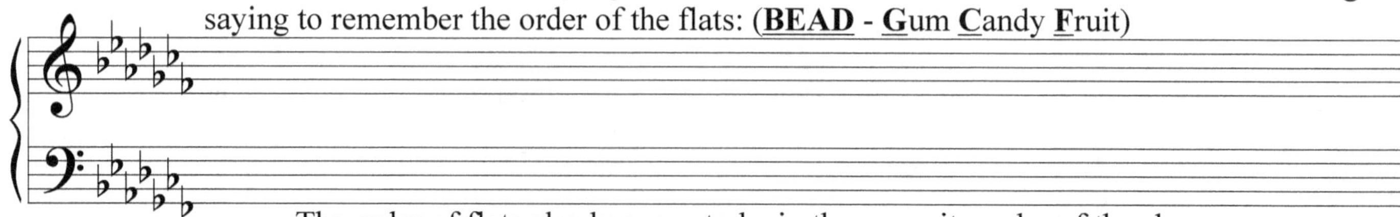

The order of flats also happens to be in the opposite order of the sharps.

IPA/Diction Review

oʊ (diphthong: 2 vowel sounds)	goat	[goʊt]	Low tongue, tip behind bottom teeth Lips open then rounded
aɪ (diphthong: 2 vowel sounds)	price	[praɪs]	Low tongue then high tongue tip behind bottom teeth then sides touching top teeth Lips tall then relaxed
ʤ	jar	[ʤɑr]	High tongue on hard palate tip behind top teeth Lips rounded
ʎ	million (but keep tongue flat, and tip behind top teeth)	[mɪljən]	High, flat tongue tip behind top teeth Lips relaxed
ʃ	ship	[ʃɪp]	High tongue sides touching top teeth Lips rounded

Sight-Singing Review

Rhythm

Melodic (with Solfege)

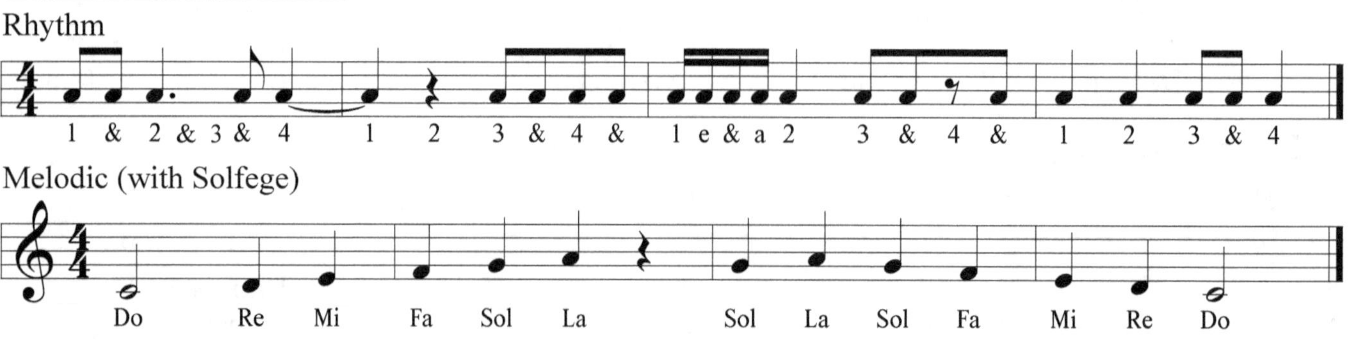

Lesson 1: Note and Rest Values

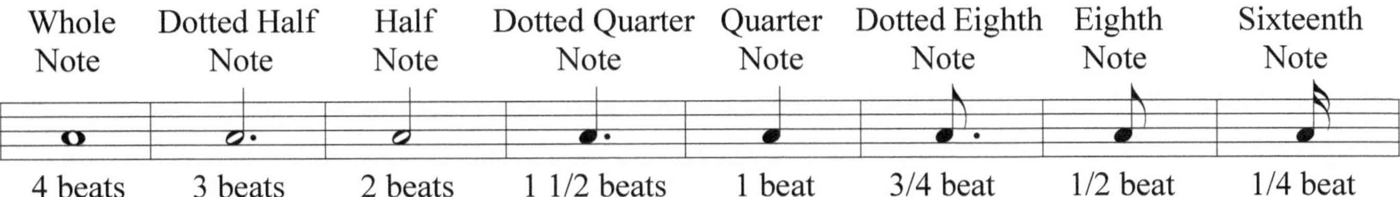

Whole Rest	Dotted Half Rest	Half Rest	Dotted Quarter Rest	Quarter Rest	Dotted Eighth Rest	Eighth Rest	Sixteenth Rest
4 beats	3 beats	2 beats	1 1/2 beats	1 beat	3/4 beat	1/2 beat	1/4 beat

Dotted Eighth Notes & Rests

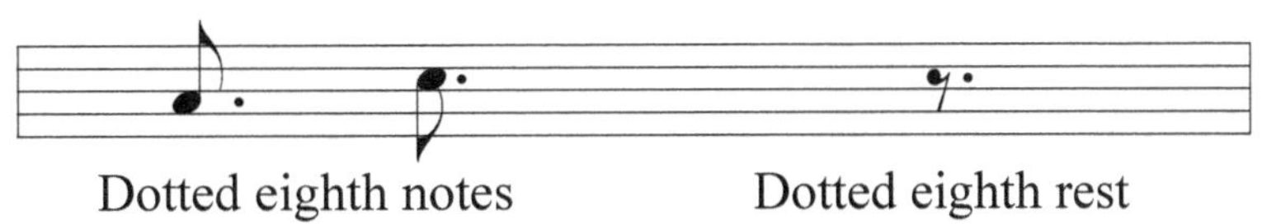

Dotted eighth notes Dotted eighth rest

A dotted eighth note is worth 3/4 of a beat in 4/4 time. Dotted eighth notes are also beamed when connected to other eighth notes or sixteenth notes.

Look at the following rhythmic examples that include dotted eighth notes.

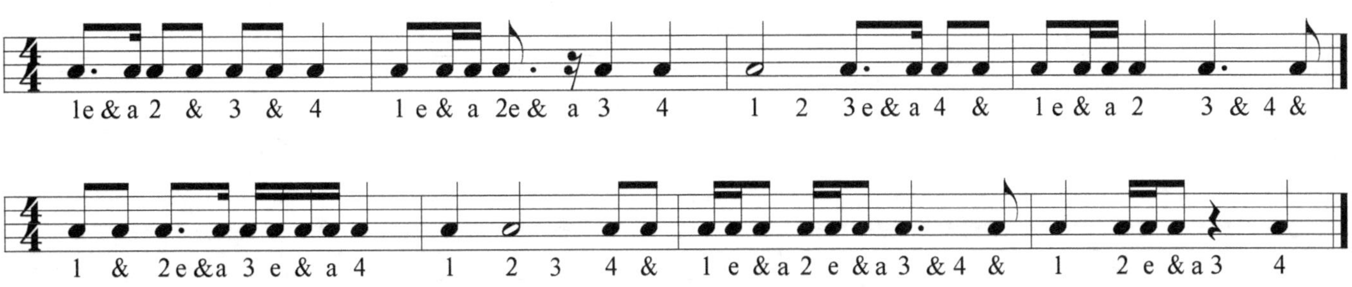

It takes 3 sixteenth notes to fit into a dotted eighth.

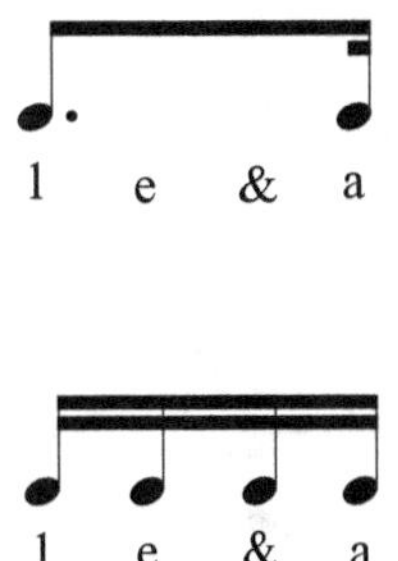

To help figure out the rhythms, it helps to say something for every note and rest we see. That's why we have 1 & 2 &, etc. Look at the examples below, and sing each measure with the beats underneath. Try to sing the rhythms in the measure while tapping a steady beat.

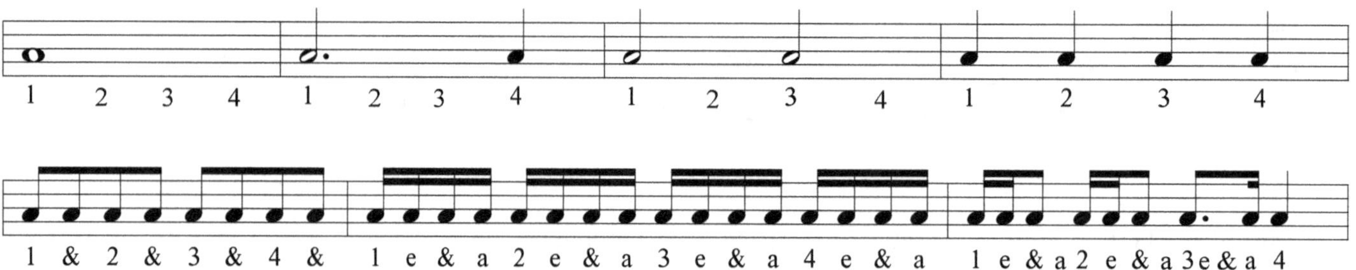

Music Rhythm Tree

Each example below shows how many of each note it takes to fill a measure. The La's indicate how to sing each note. If you see "La - - -" that means you are holding the note for more than one beat.

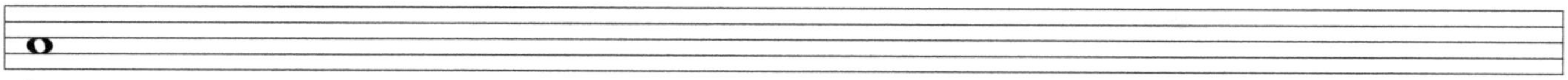

1 2 3 4
La - - -

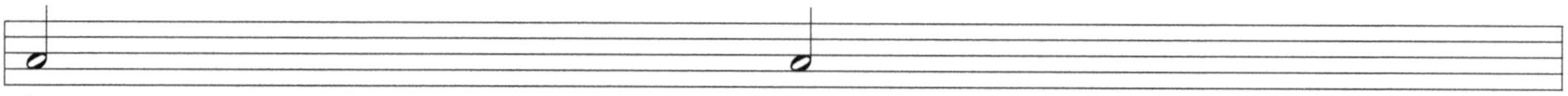

1 2 3 4
La - La -

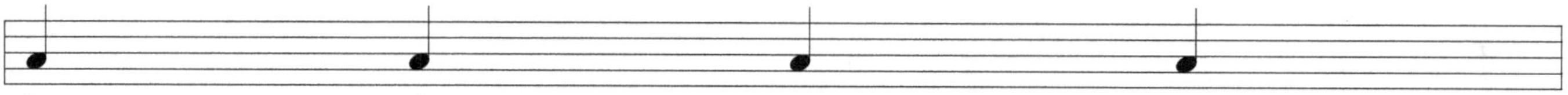

1 2 3 4
La La La La

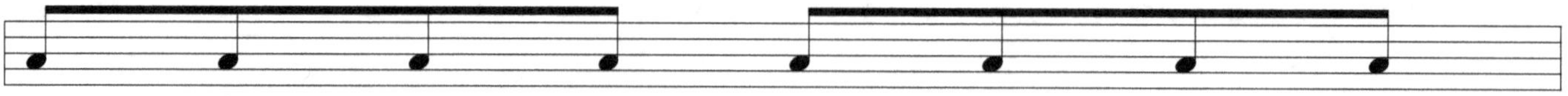

1 & 2 & 3 & 4 &
La La La La La La La La

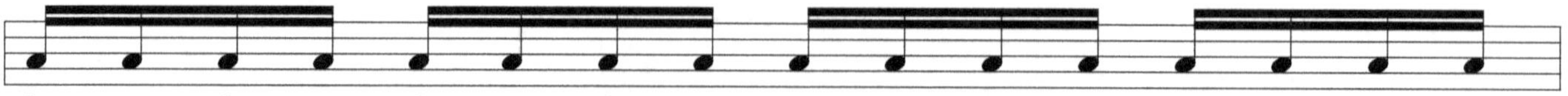

1 e & a 2 e & a 3 e & a 4 e & a
La La La La La La La La La La La La La La La La

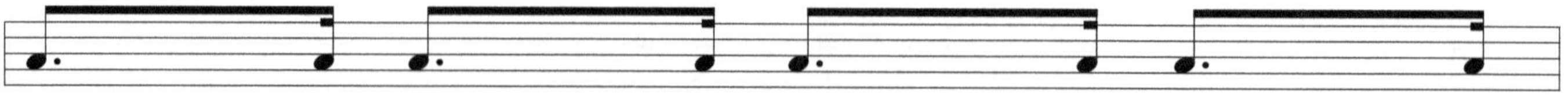

1 e & a 2 e & a 3 e & a 4 e & a
La - - La La - - La La - - La La - - La

Review: Lesson 1

1. Check the correct counting for each of these examples.

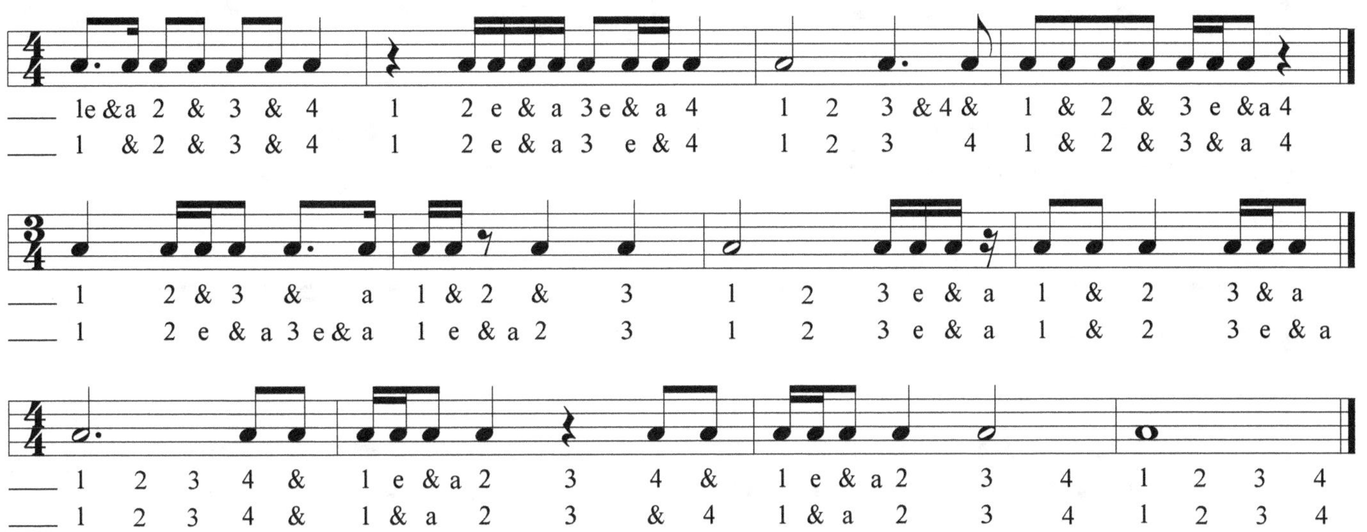

2. Check the correct number of beats each note or rest will receive in $\frac{4}{4}$ time.

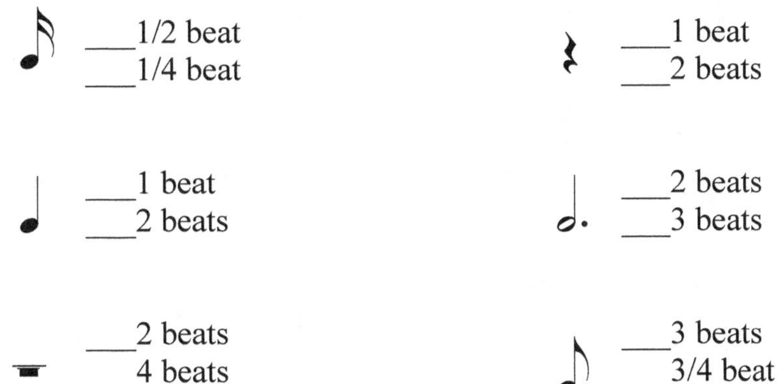

3. Circle the correct name for each note or rest.

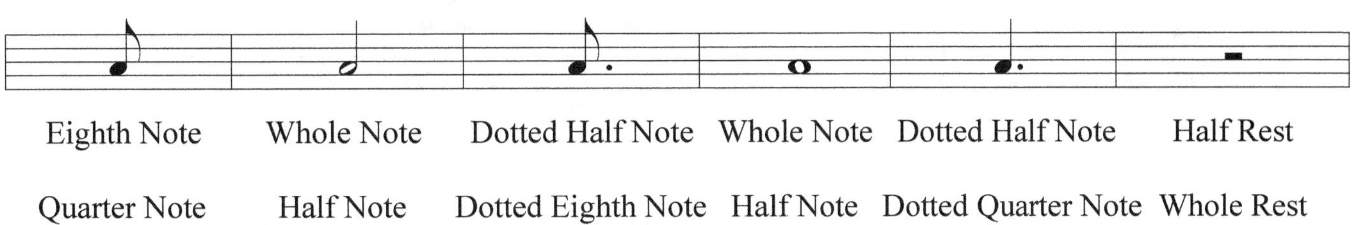

4. Write the beats under the notes, then add missing bar lines and a double bar line to each example.

5. Add the missing time signature to the following examples.

6. Add **one** missing note or rest to each measure.

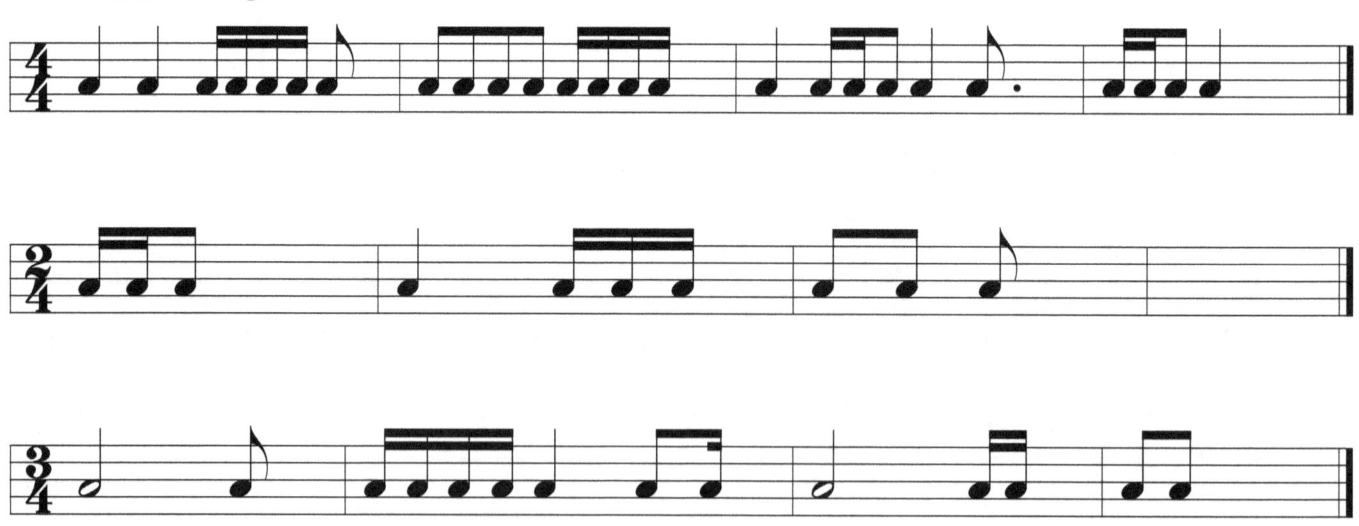

7. Write the beats under the notes/rests in each example, then write La's according to how you would sing the notes. You can use dashes to indicate held notes. The first example is done for you.

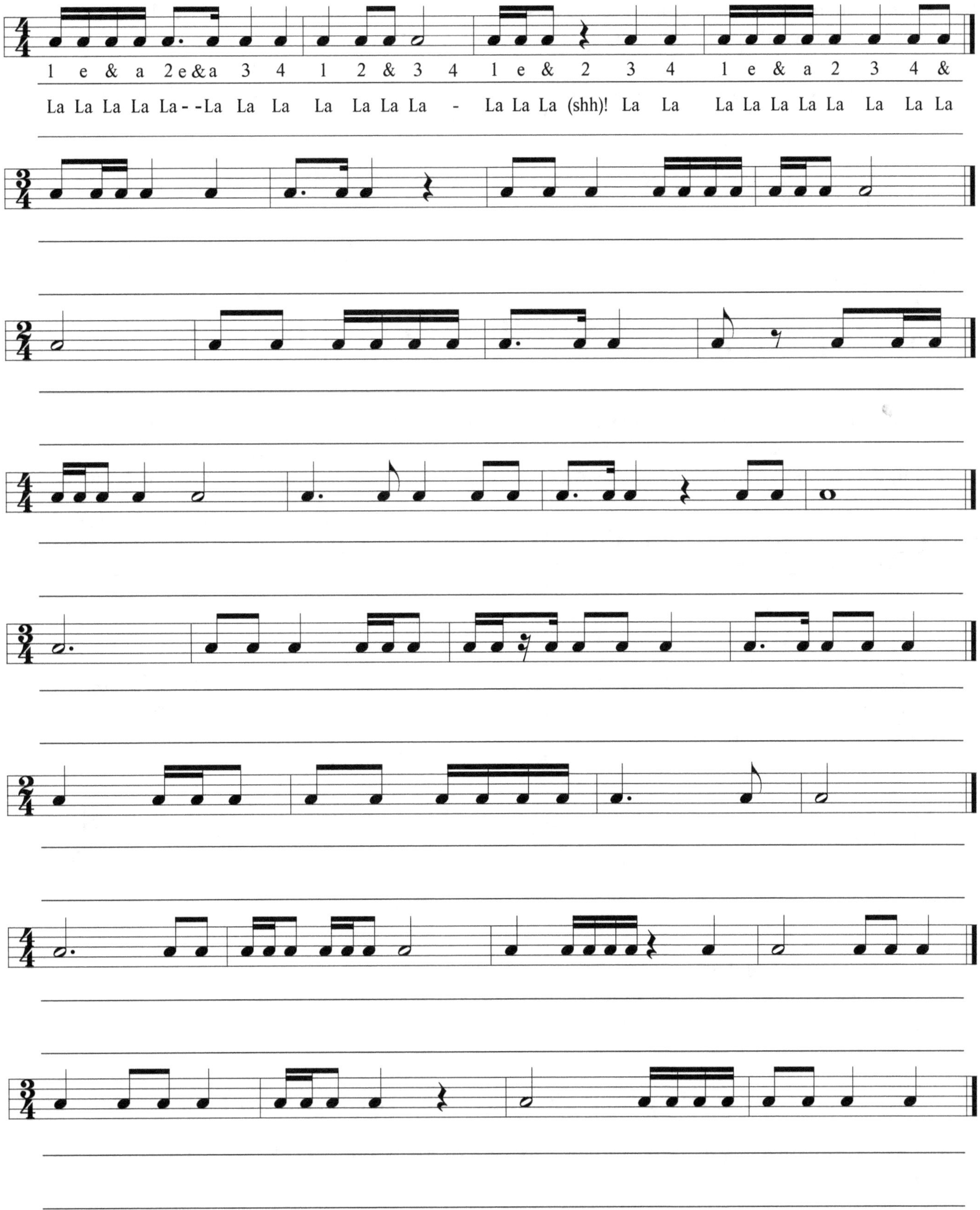

Lesson 2: Primary Triads

In Levels 1-4, triads (3-note chords) were built on the first note of the scale. If an example was in the key of E Major, then the triad introduced was an E Major triad, with E (root), G♯ (middle) and B (top). In this lesson, you'll learn that triads are also built on the other seven notes of the scale.

In the example below, there is a triad built on every note of the E Major scale, and the sharps belonging to E Major (F♯, C♯, G♯, D♯) have been added.

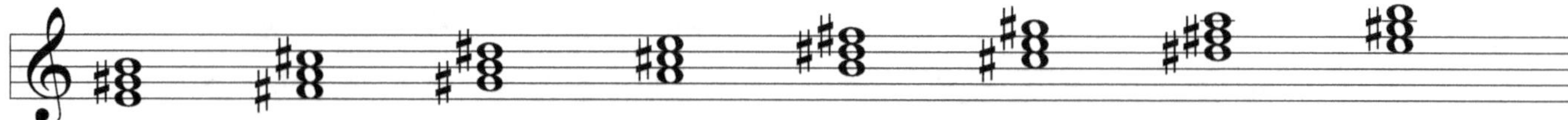

In this example, there is an E Major key signature added, so sharps do not have to be written on the chords themselves.

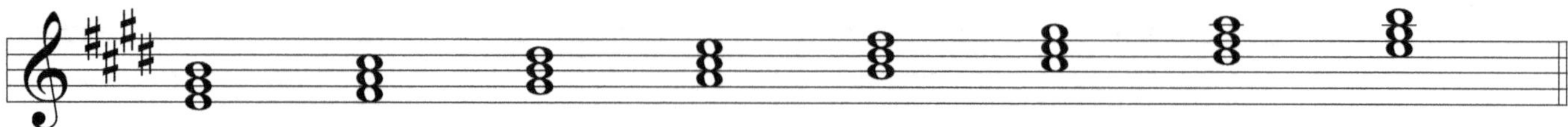

In music, the triads in a scale are identified or numbered with Roman Numerals. The Major triads are given upper case Roman Numerals and the minor* triads are given lower case Roman Numerals.The example below shows triads in the key of E Major with their corresponding Roman Numeral numbers.

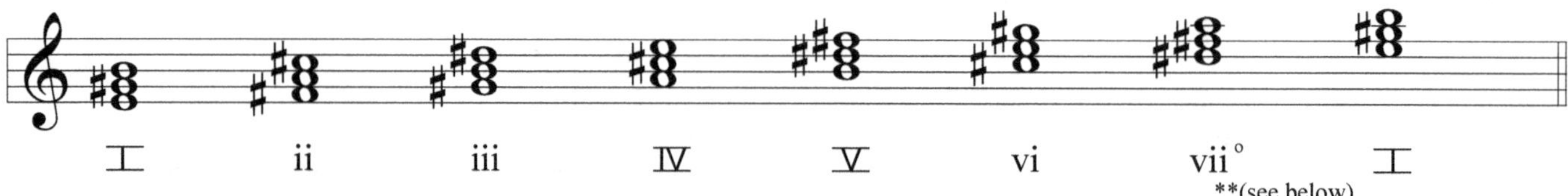

In a Major key, the Major triads are the I, IV, & V . These triads are known as the **Primary Triads**. These three chords happen to be the most important and commonly used accompaniment chords in classical music and in today's contemporary music.
The example below shows the primary triads in the key of E Major.

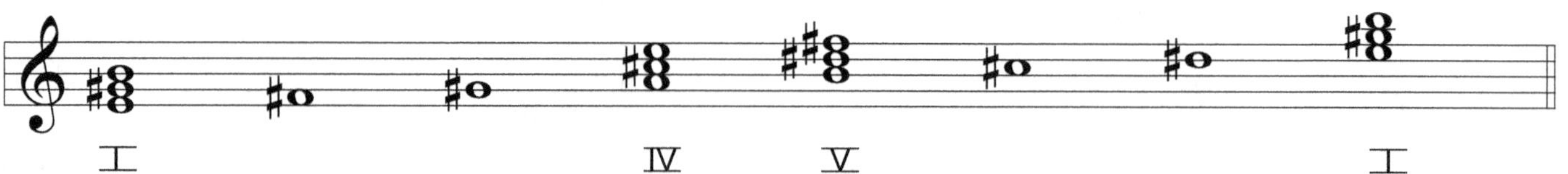

The I chord is called the **Tonic**.
The IV chord is called the **Subdominant**.
The V chord is called the **Dominant**.

*Minor key signatures and chords will be introduced later in this chapter.

**The ° is a symbol that indicates a diminished chord. In a diminished chord, the top and middle notes have been lowered by a half step. This concept is covered in Level 6.

Here are some well known tunes with the primary triad chord progression (I-IV -V) in the accompaniment. You can also listen to "Twist and Shout" by the Beatles, "La Bamba" by Ritchie Valens, or just about any song from the 1950's for more examples of this chord progressoion.

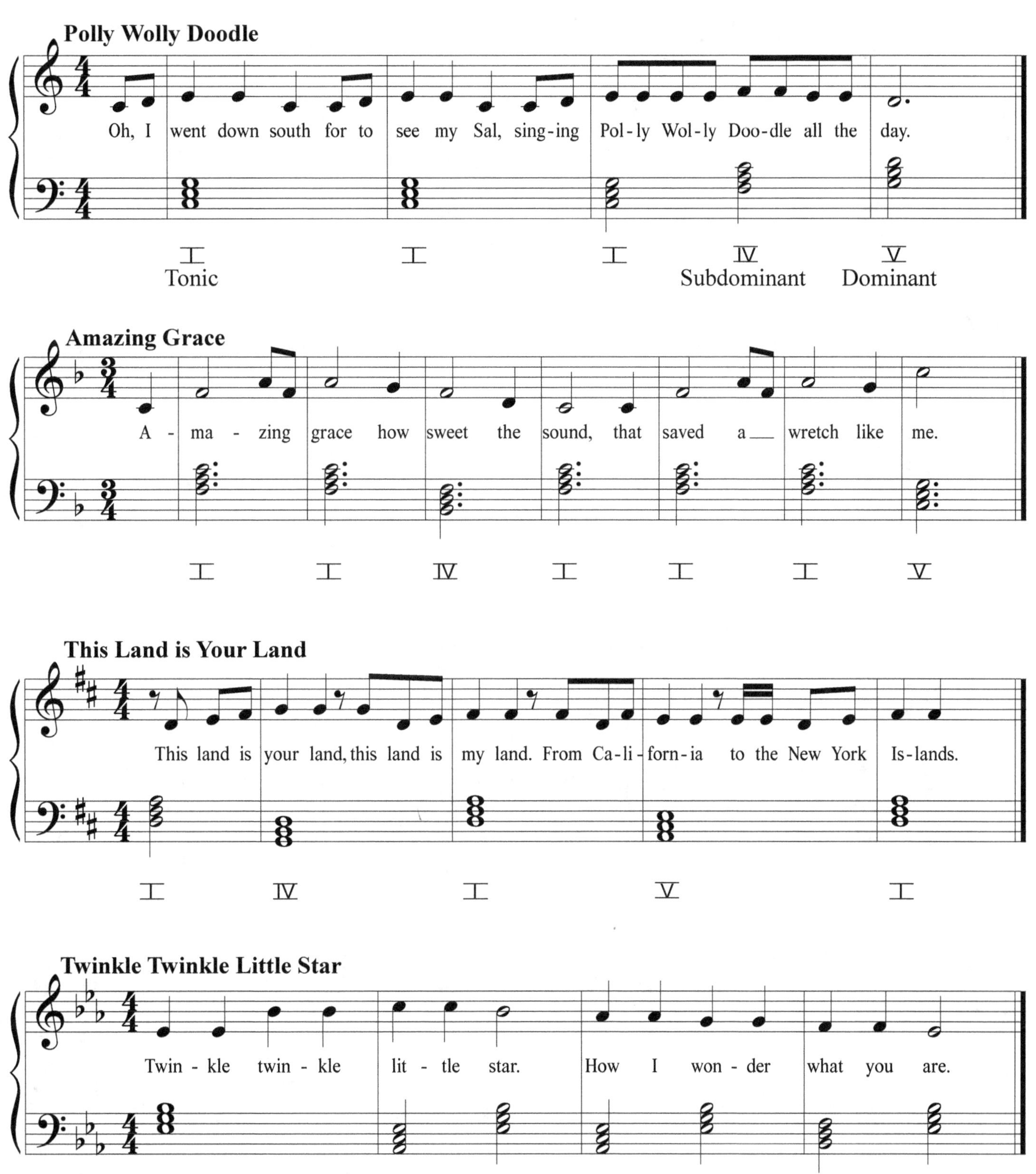

Remember, the primary triads are built on the I (Do), IV (Fa) and V (Sol).
Below are the primary triads in all the Major keys.

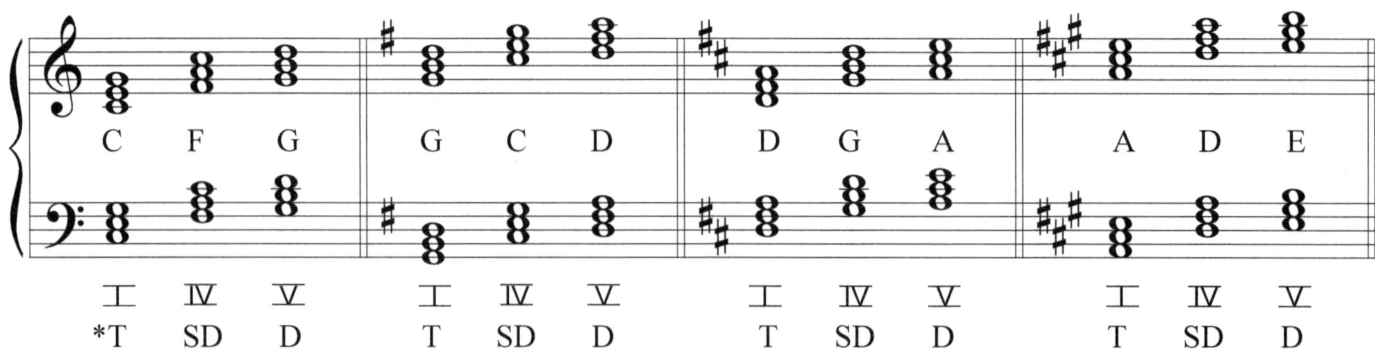

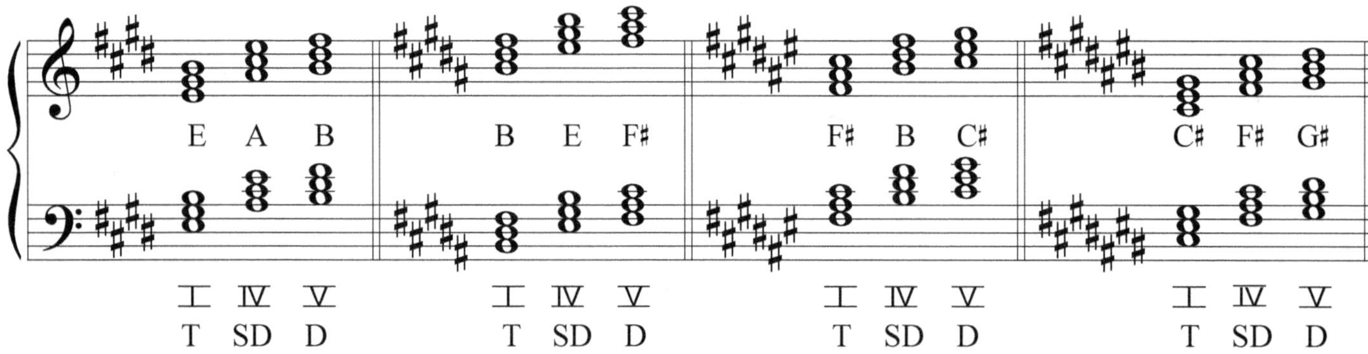

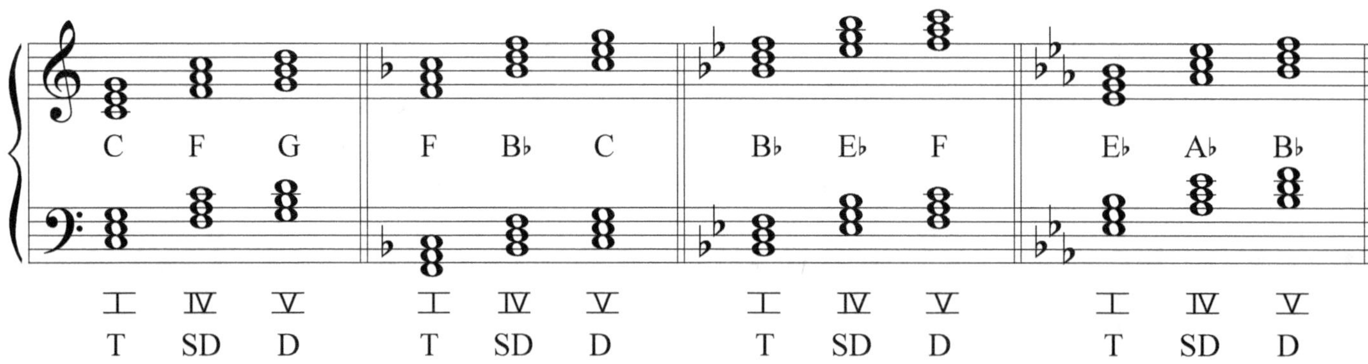

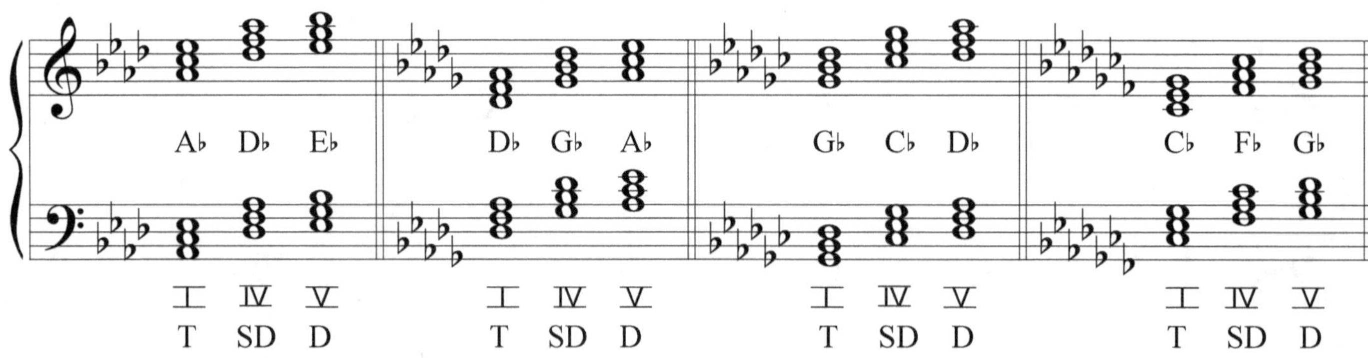

*T=Tonic, SD=Subdominant, D=Dominant

Review: Lesson 2

1. Check the name for the following Roman numerals.

a. I ___ Dominant
___ Tonic

b. IV ___ Dominant
___ Subdominant

c. V ___ Dominant
___ Tonic

2. Check the Roman numeral for each triad in the following keys.

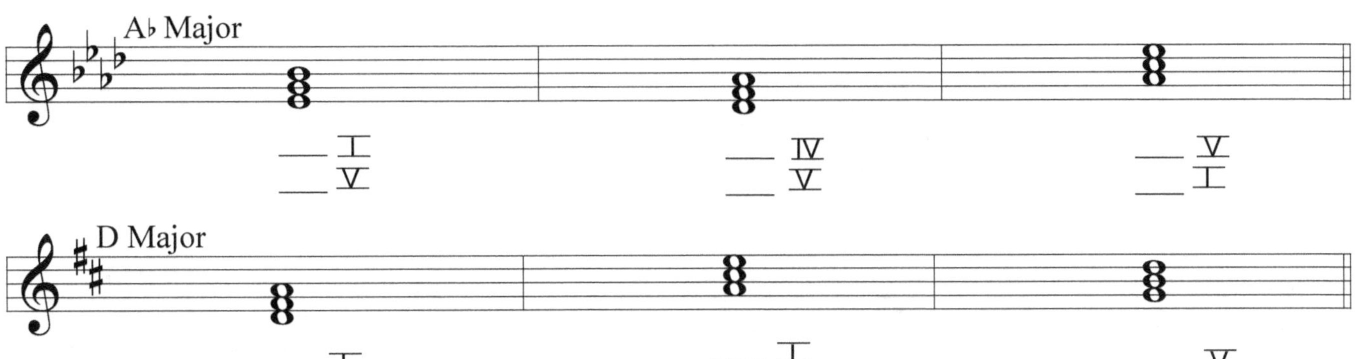

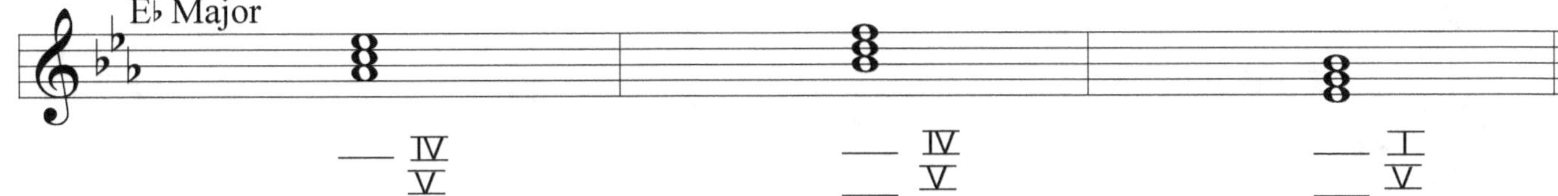

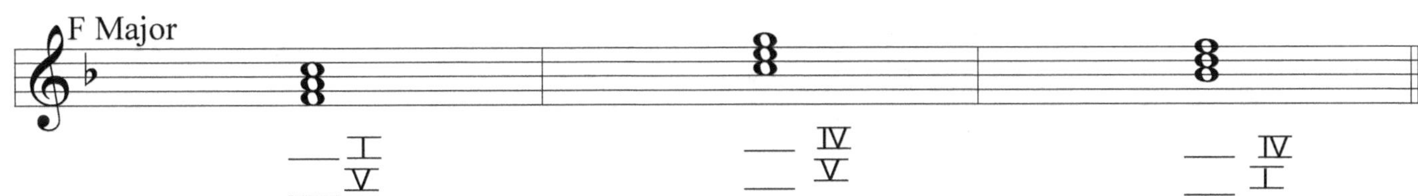

3. Circle the primary triads (I, IV, V) in each example, then label them with the correct Roman Numerals.

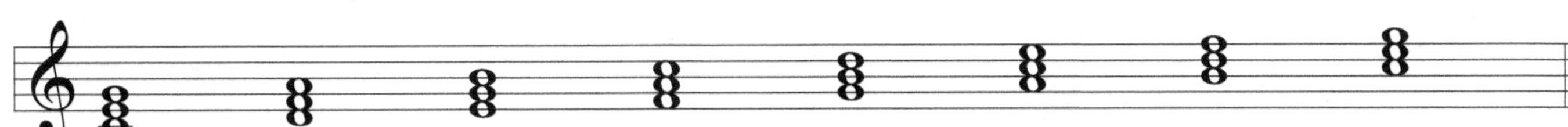

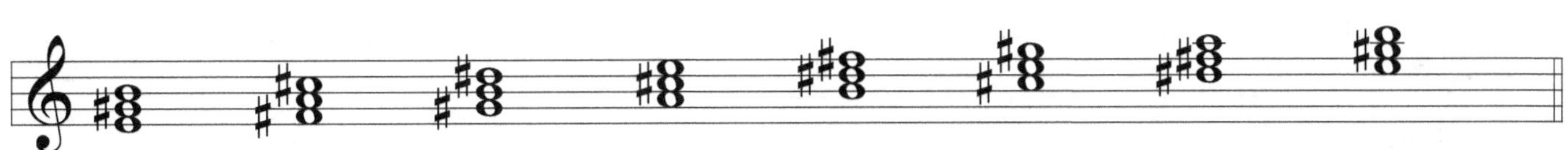

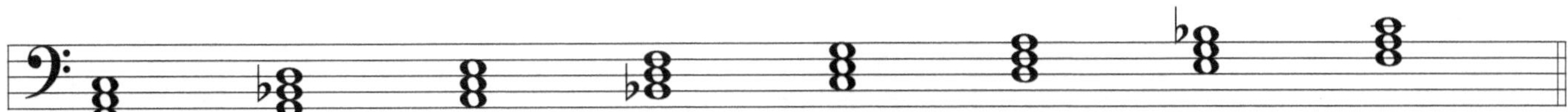

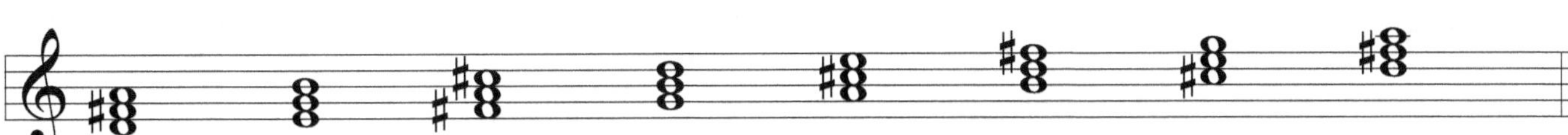

4. On the Major scales below:
   a. Add the Roman Numerals (I, IV, V) to the appropriate notes.
   b. Create a primary triad on the first, fourth, fifth & eighth notes of the scale.
   c. Do not write a key signature.
   d. Add any additional sharps/flats according to the key that is given. The first one is done for you.

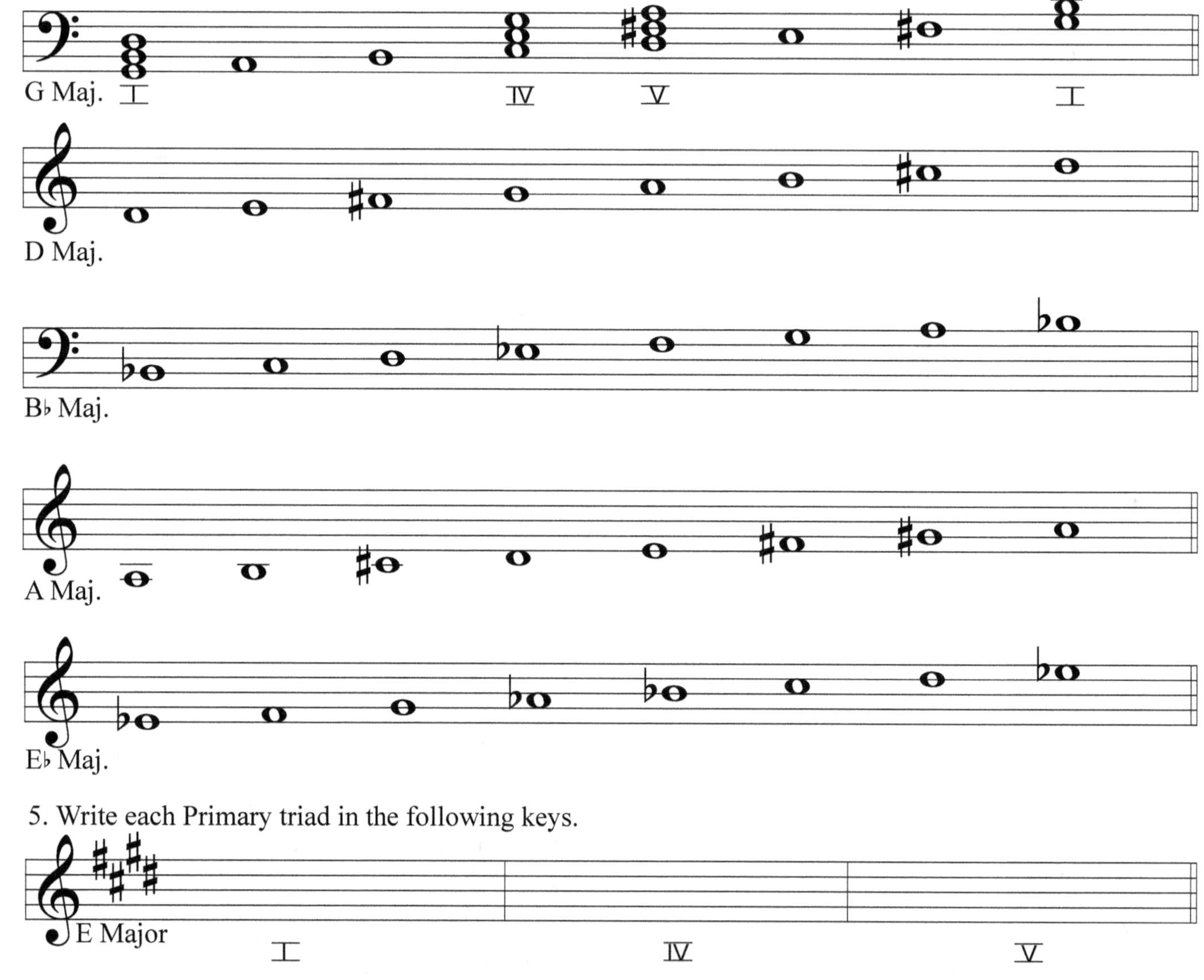

5. Write each Primary triad in the following keys.

F Major
I IV V

G Major
I IV V

6. Circle the Primary triads in the examples (piano accompaniment) below and label them with the correct Roman Numerals. Write the name of the Major key in the space provided as well. Remember, the lowest note in the Tonic (Ⅰ) chord is the same as the key the example is in. So, if the example is in D Major, then a D chord (Tonic) would have a D, F# & A.

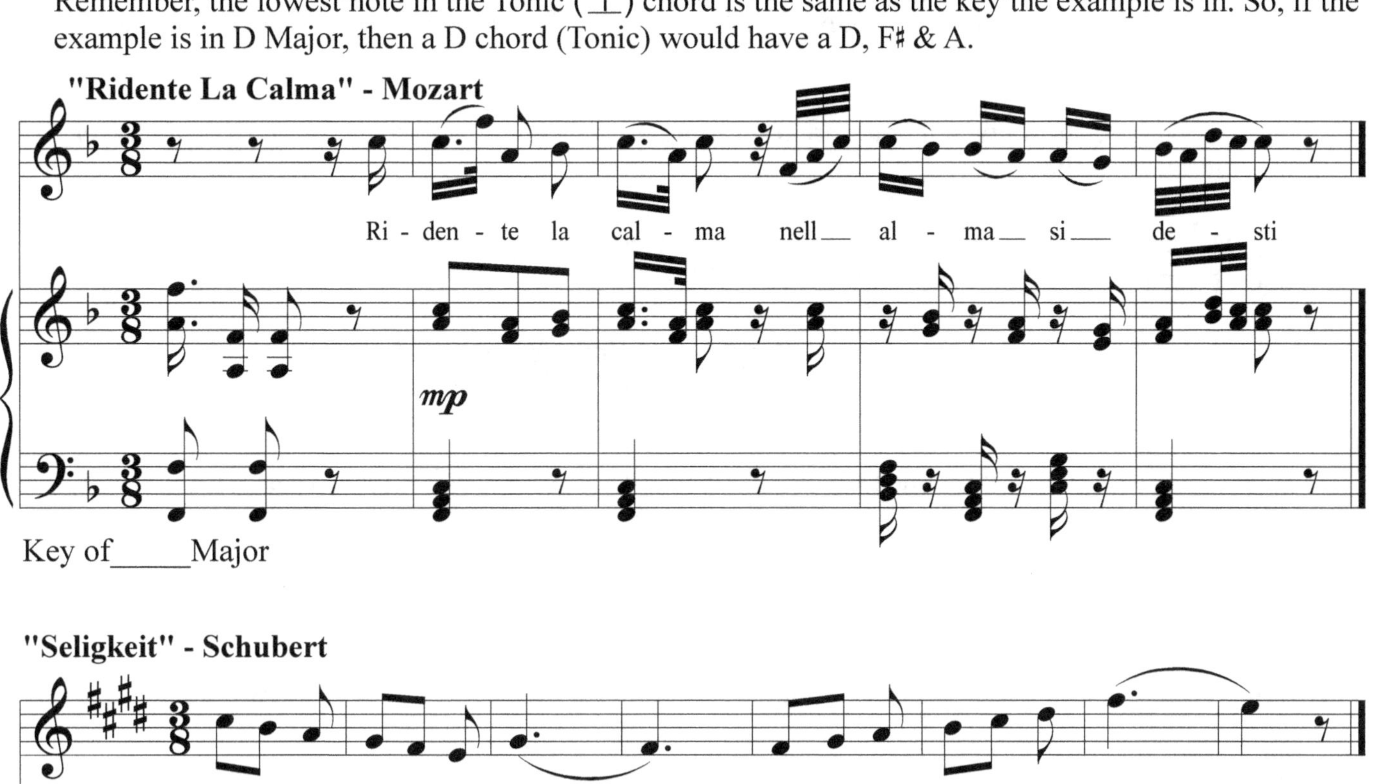

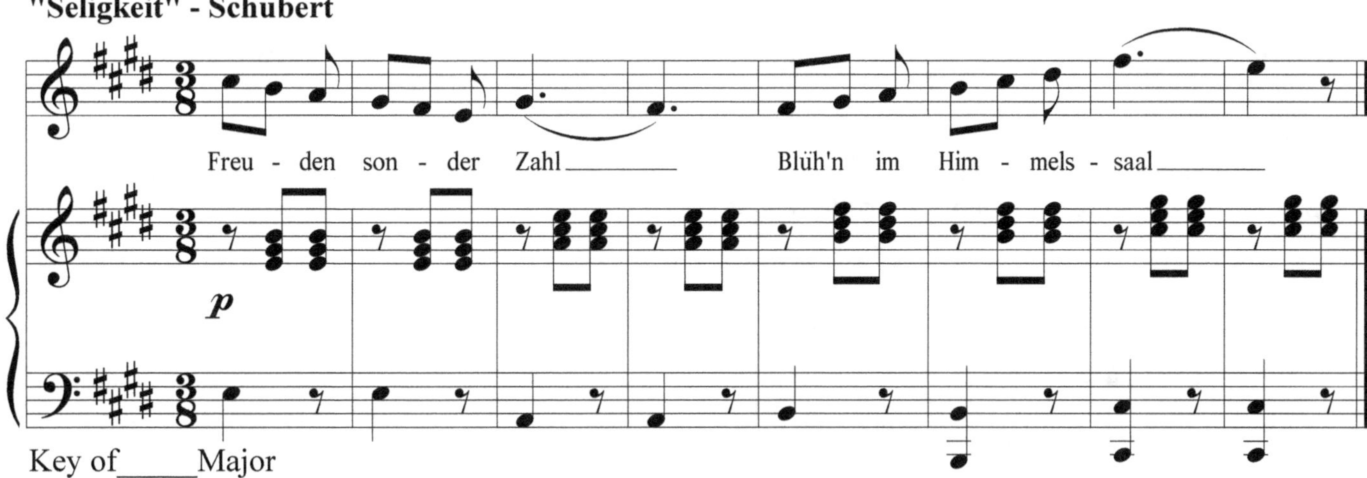

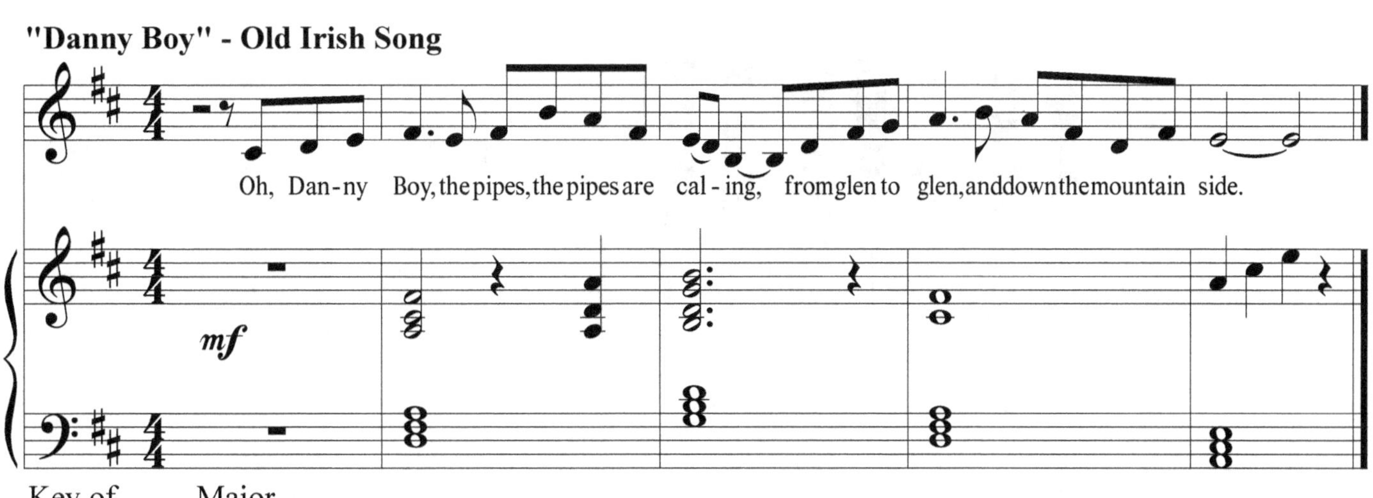

Lesson 3: Minor Key Signatures

In music, a Key Signature is a series of sharp (♯) or flat (♭) symbols placed on the staff immediately after the Treble and Bass clefs. The Key Signature also creates the tonal center (Do) for a piece. If a piece is in D Major, D is Do.

The key signature shows which notes are to be sung a half step higher (sharp) or a half step lower (flat) for the duration of the piece.

Every Major key has a "relative" minor key. The easiest way to understand the difference between the sound of songs in a Major and minor key is:

Major key = Happy   minor key = Sad

In order for a scale to be in a minor key, the notes must follow a specific pattern of half steps and whole steps.

The pattern of half steps and whole steps that make up a <u>minor</u> scale (8 notes) is as follows:

Whole - Half - Whole - Whole - Half - Whole - Whole   (W - H - W - W - H - W - W)

Take a look at an e minor scale on the staff below. The F♯ must be added in order for the formula (pattern of half steps and whole steps) to be correct.

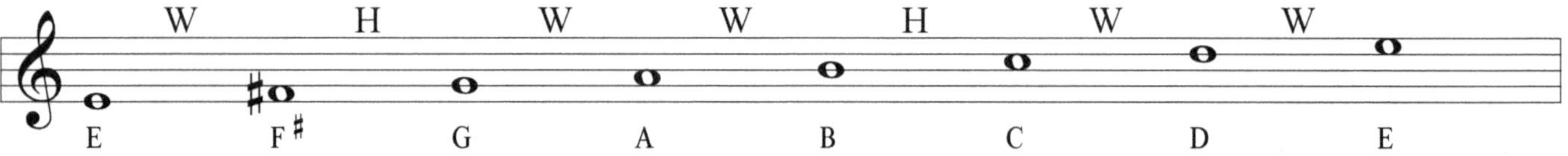

Here is what an e minor scale looks like on a piano keyboard.

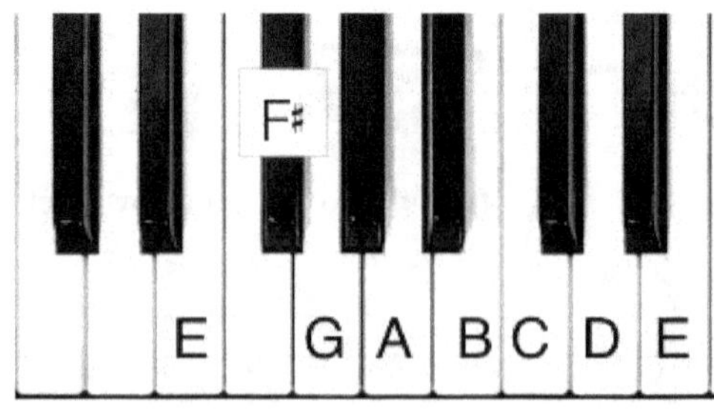

-E to F♯ is a whole step
(there is a white note in between)
-F♯ to G is a half step
-G to A is a whole step
-A to B is a whole step
-B to C is a half step (no note in between, they are as close as they can be
-C to D is a whole step
-D to E is a whole step

*Remember the "natural half steps" between B-C and E-F. These pitches are right next to each other. Look at the keyboard above to see how close they are on a piano!

Every Major key is related to a minor key because they share the same key signature (sharps/flats). For instance, F Major and d minor are related because they both have a B♭ in the key signature. If you sing a scale starting on F (as Do) F-G-A-B♭-C-D-E-F, it will sound happy (Major). If you sing the same scale starting on D (as Do) D-E-F-G-A-B♭-C-D, it will sound sad (minor).

There are **two** ways to find a Major key's relative minor key.

1. The relative minor key (Do) is the 6th note of a Major key's scale. In solfege, this is the "La."

2. The relative minor key is a minor 3rd (3 half steps) lower than the Major Key's Do.

Look at the following example. D (La) is the 6th note of the F Major Scale. It is the relative minor key.

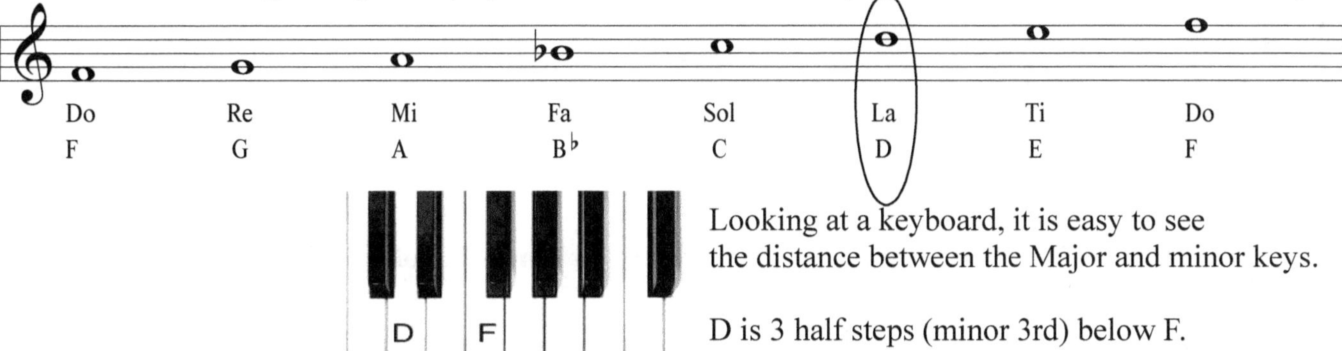

Looking at a keyboard, it is easy to see the distance between the Major and minor keys.

D is 3 half steps (minor 3rd) below F.

Here are four Major keys and their relative minor keys.

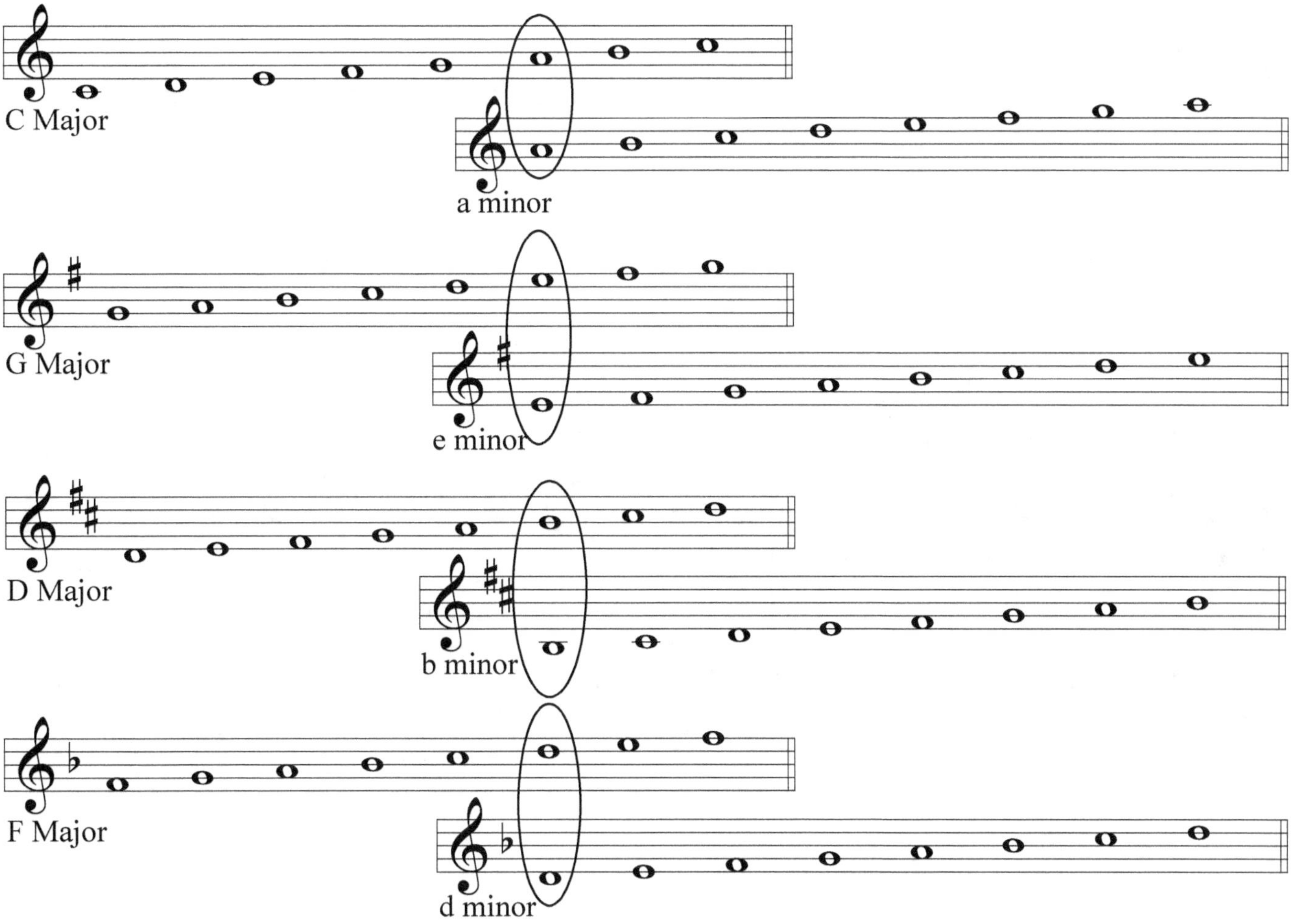

C Major

a minor

G Major

e minor

D Major

b minor

F Major

d minor

Here are some familiar melodies in minor keys.

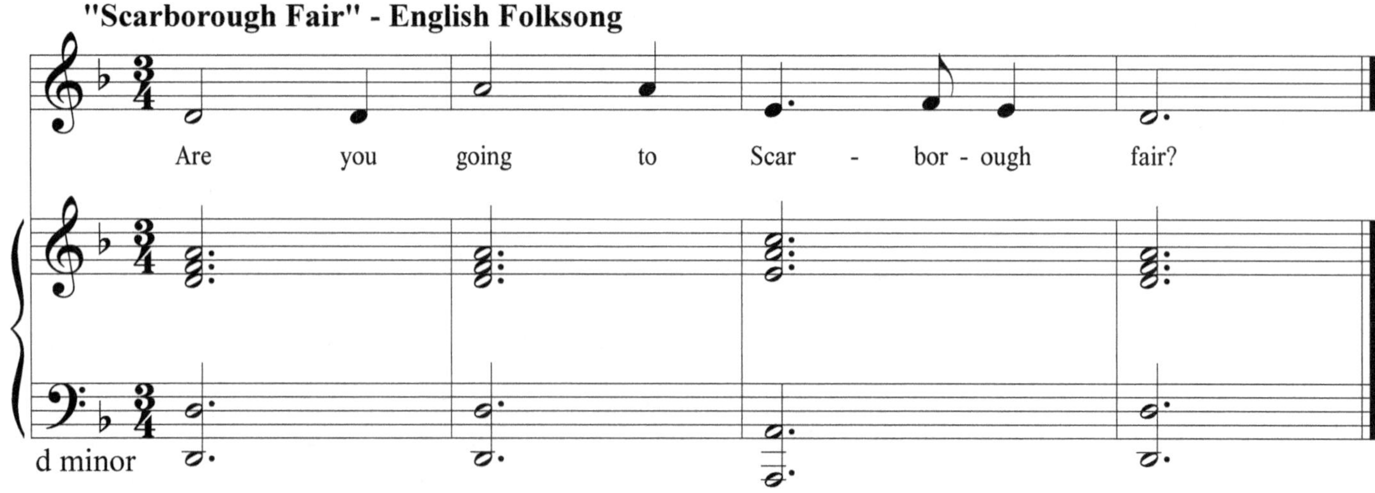

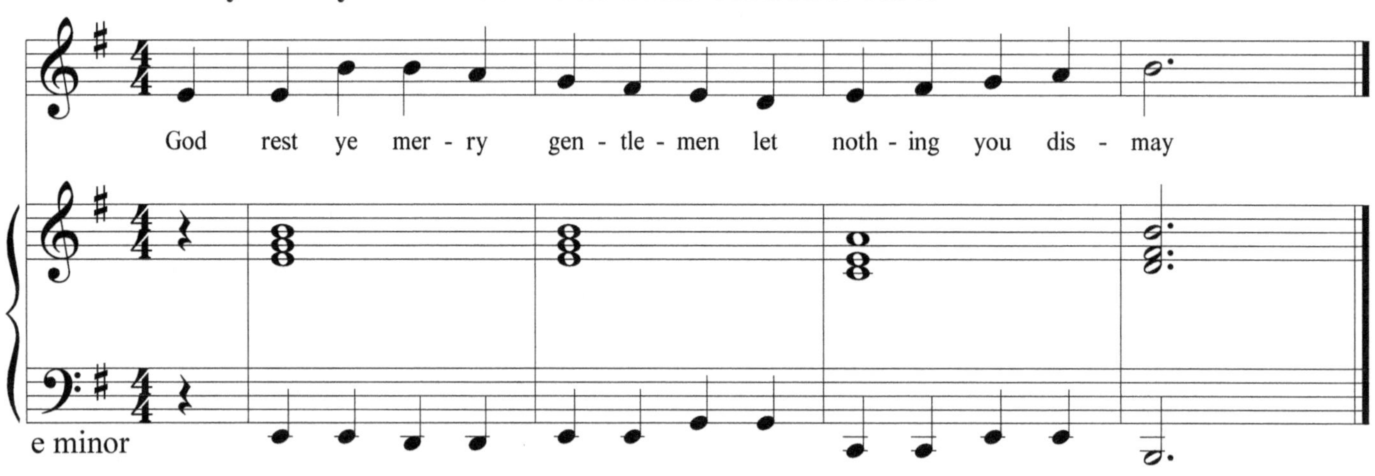

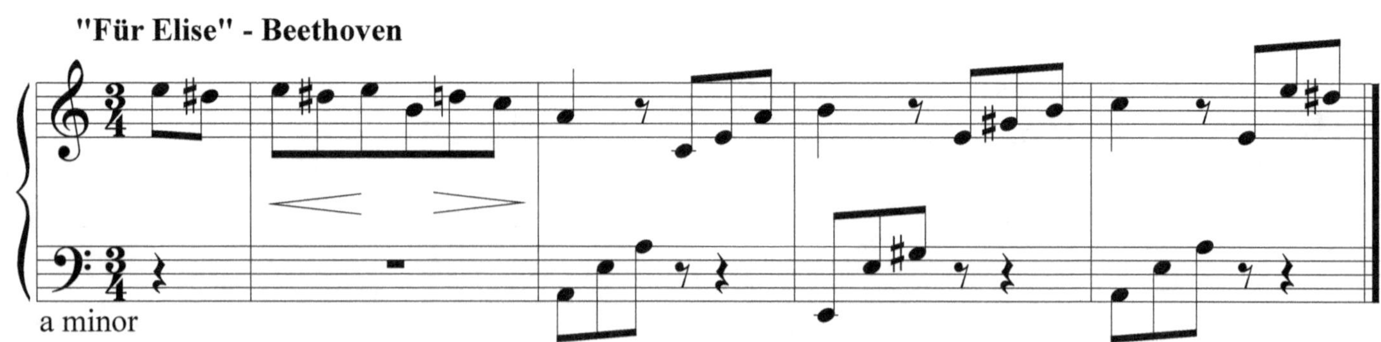

Review: Lesson 3

1. Circle the correct pattern of Whole steps and Half steps that create a minor scale.

   a. W W H W W W H

   b. W H W W H W W

2. Check the correct answer for the following:

   a. A relative minor key shares the same ___________ as the Major Key. ___sharps/flats ___name

   b. You can find the relative minor key by looking at the _____ of the Major scale. ___Fa ___La

   c. Songs in a minor key sound _______ while Major keys sound _________. ___sad/happy ___happy/sad

3. Fill in the relative minor key for each of the Major keys listed. Refer to the piano to count down 3 half steps to find the minor key, or go to the La of the scale.

   C Major - ____ minor   G Major - ____ minor

   F Major - ____ minor   D Major - ____ minor

4. Circle the relative minor note (La) in each of these Major scales.

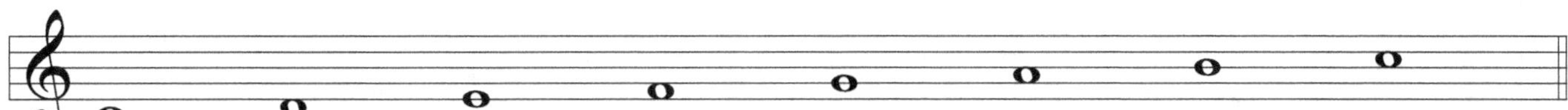

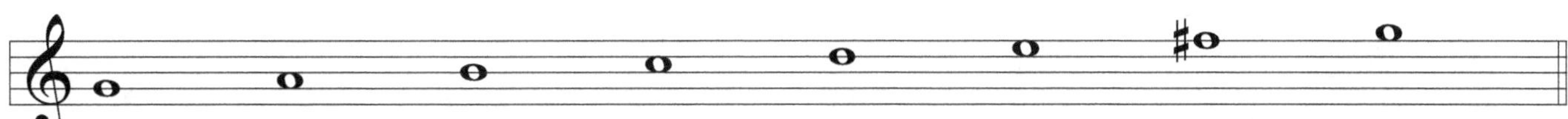

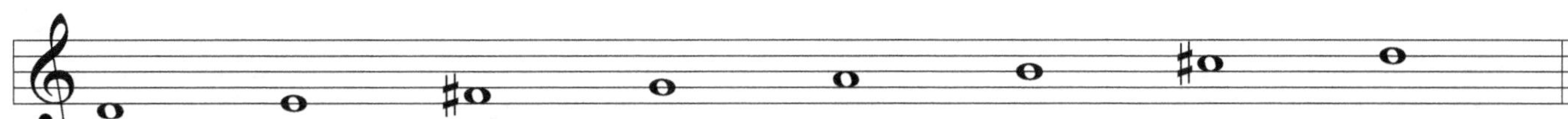

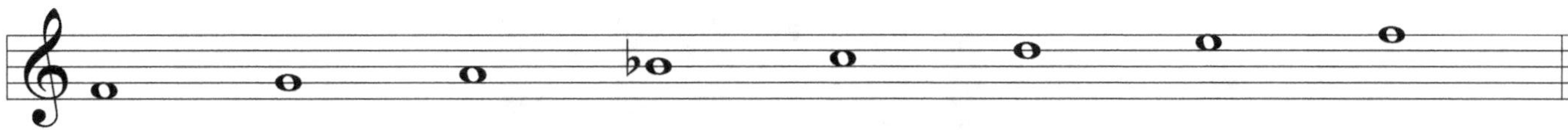

5. Add the necessary ♯ or ♭ to the scales below to create **minor** scales. Make sure you draw the ♯/♭ before the note that is affected. The center part of the sharp and flat must be on the same line/space of the note it is affecting. **Do not use a key signature.** It helps to think of the key signature for the relative Major key, then add the same ♯/♭ to the minor scale. Use the keyboard below to find the relative Major from the minor by going up three half-steps.

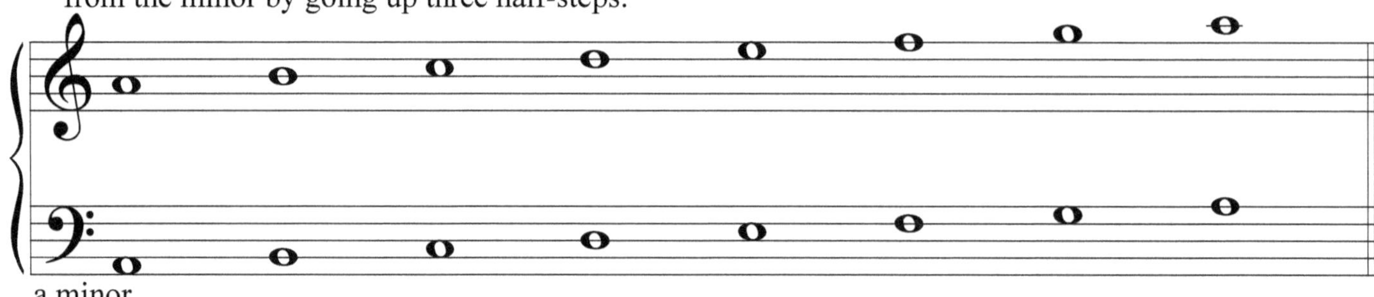

a minor

e minor

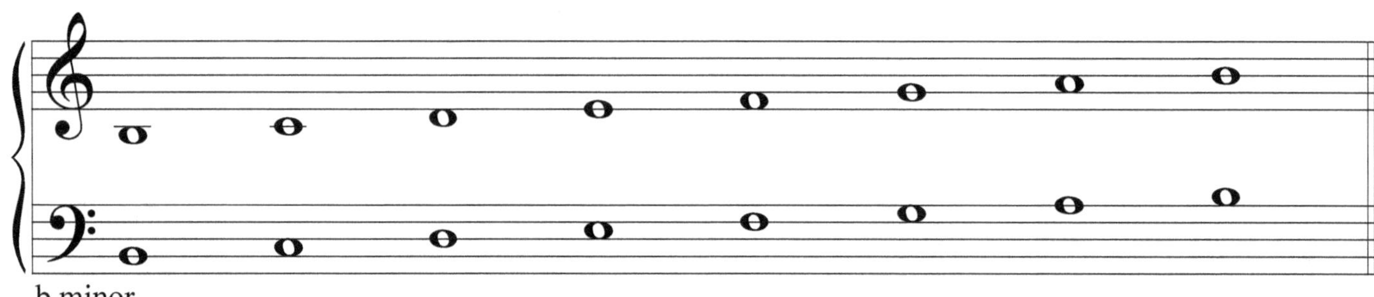

b minor

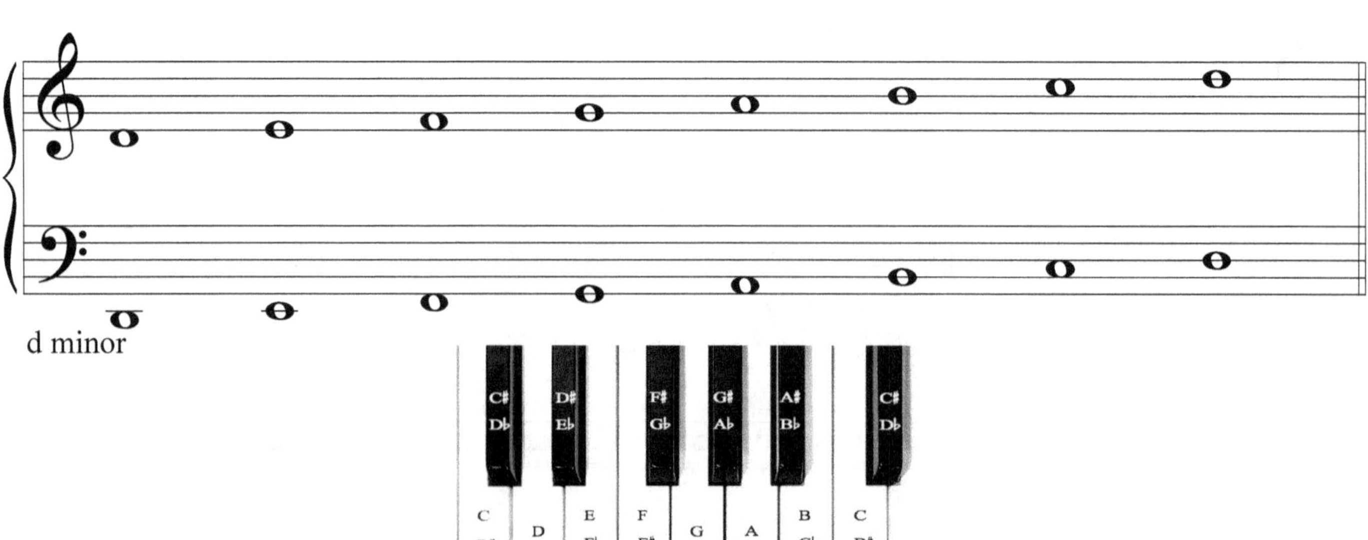

6. What is the order of sharps in a key signature?

____ ____ ____ ____ ____ ____ ____

7. What saying can be used to remember the order of sharps?

____

8. What is the order of flats in a key signature?

____ ____ ____ ____ ____ ____ ____

9. What saying can be used to remember the order of flats?

____

10. The order of sharps is in the______________________order than the order of flats.

11. Draw the sharps 2 times, in order, on both the treble and bass staves. Be careful that the center part of the sharp is on the correct line or space.

12. Draw the flats 2 times, in order, on both the treble and bass staves. Be careful that the center part of the flat is on the correct line or space.

13. Name the sharps, in order in the following keys. The first one is done for you.

F♯, C♯

14. Name the flats, in order in the following keys. The first one is done for you.

B♭, E♭

15. For the following examples:

-Determine the key (and whether it is Major or minor). Hint: Look at the starting and ending notes to see if it centers around the Major or minor key.

-Write the note names underneath the notes. Be sure to add the ♯/♭ if the note is affected by the key signature. Watch the clef changes - it may help to circle the Bass clefs so you don't forget! The first measure is done for you.

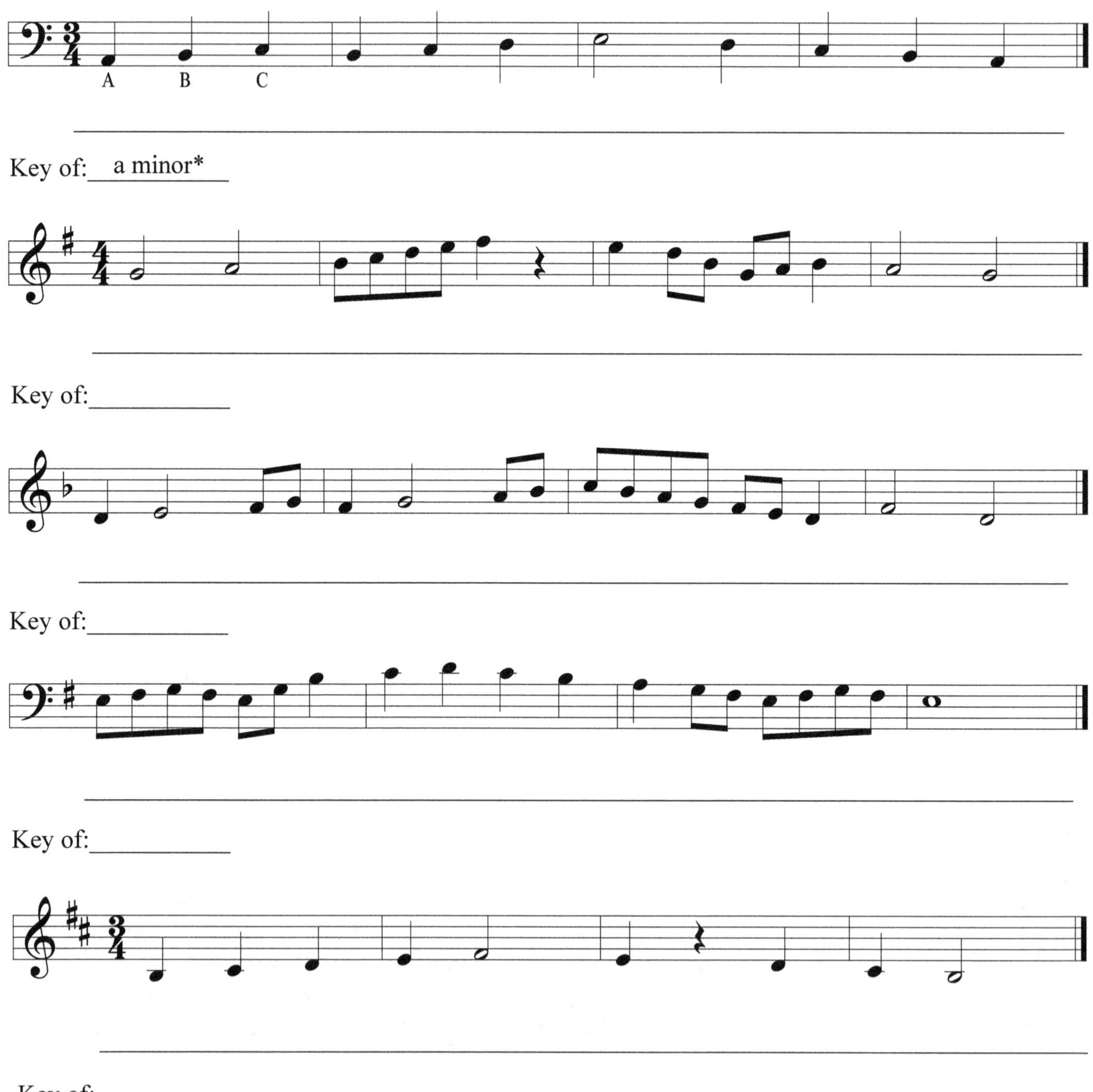

*starts and ends on an A, so in this example, A is "Do."

16. Name the following **Major** key signatures. Don't forget to add a ♯/♭ in the chord name, if necessary. The first one is done for you.

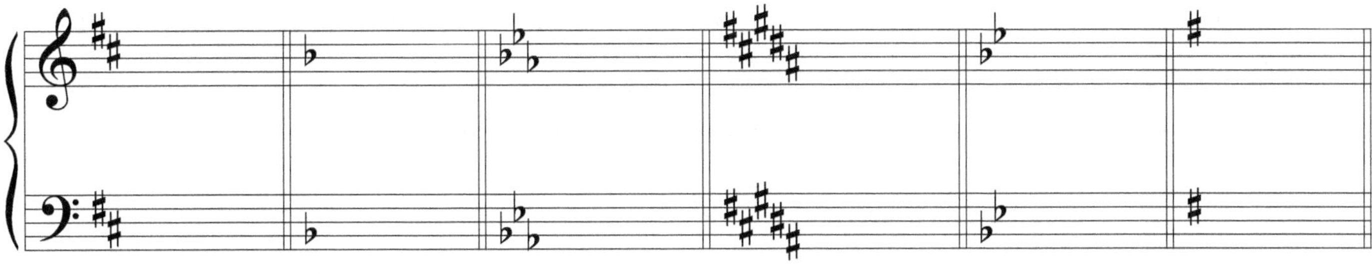

D Major

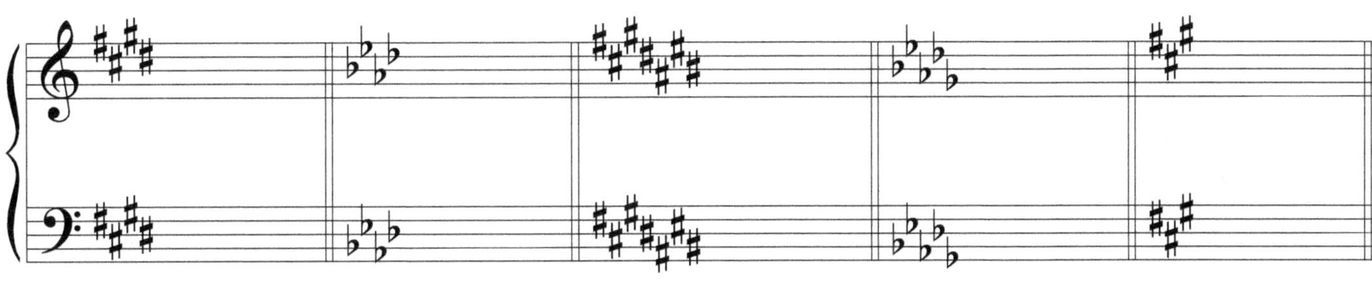

17. Name the following **minor** key signatures.

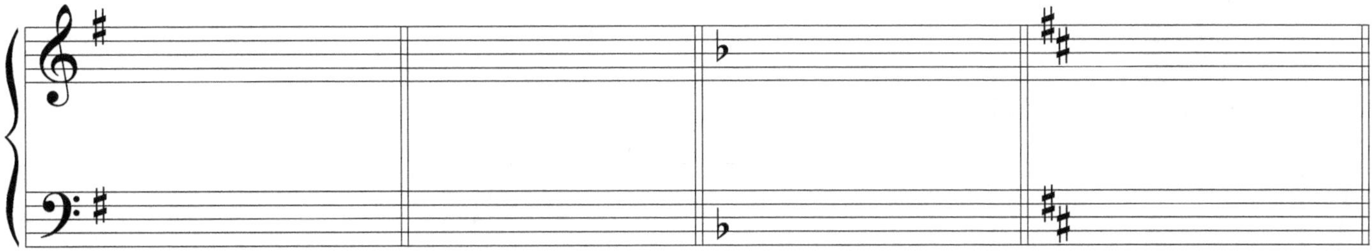

Lesson 4: Minor Triads

A **Triad**, or 3-note chord, is formed when the first, third and fifth notes of a scale are sung or played, either consecutively or at the same time. The root, or the lowest note of a triad, determines its letter name.

Example d minor d is the 1st/root, f is the 3rd/middle note, a is the 5th/top note

This is a "root position" chord.

The following examples show the minor scales and minor triads formed on the first note of the scale (Do). The 1st, 3rd, and 5th notes (Do-Mi-Sol) are circled.

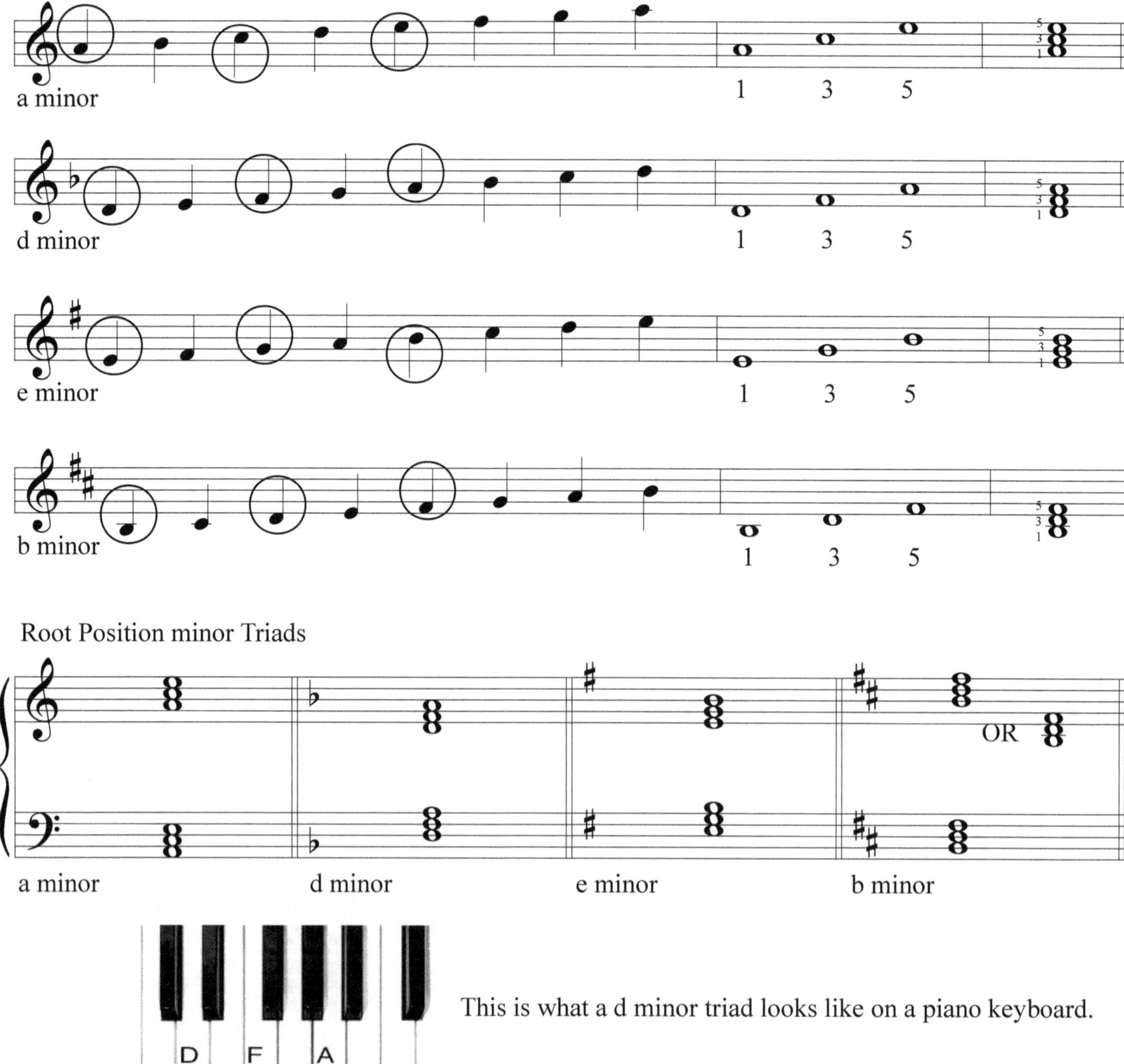

This is what a d minor triad looks like on a piano keyboard.

Review: Lesson 4

1. Name the following minor triads. Remember, look at the bottom note (root) for the "name" of the triad.

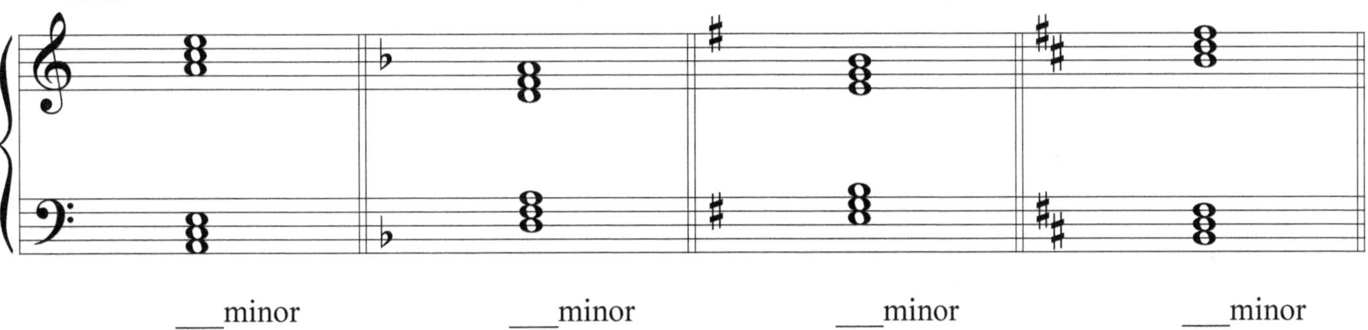

___minor ___minor ___minor ___minor

2. The following triads are in the relative Major keys to the above minor triads. Name each Major triad.

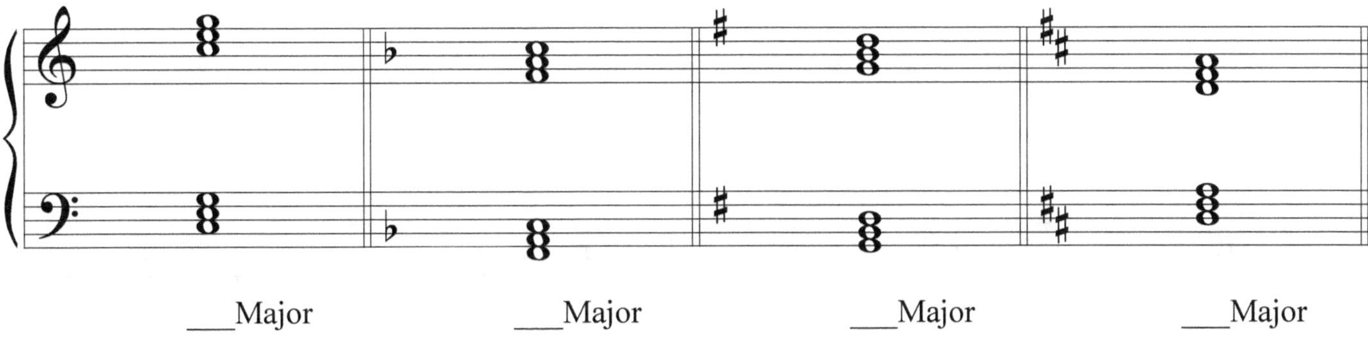

___Major ___Major ___Major ___Major

3. For the following examples, draw the correct key signature, then add the root position triads to both the Treble and Bass clefs. Look at question 1 & 2 for hints.

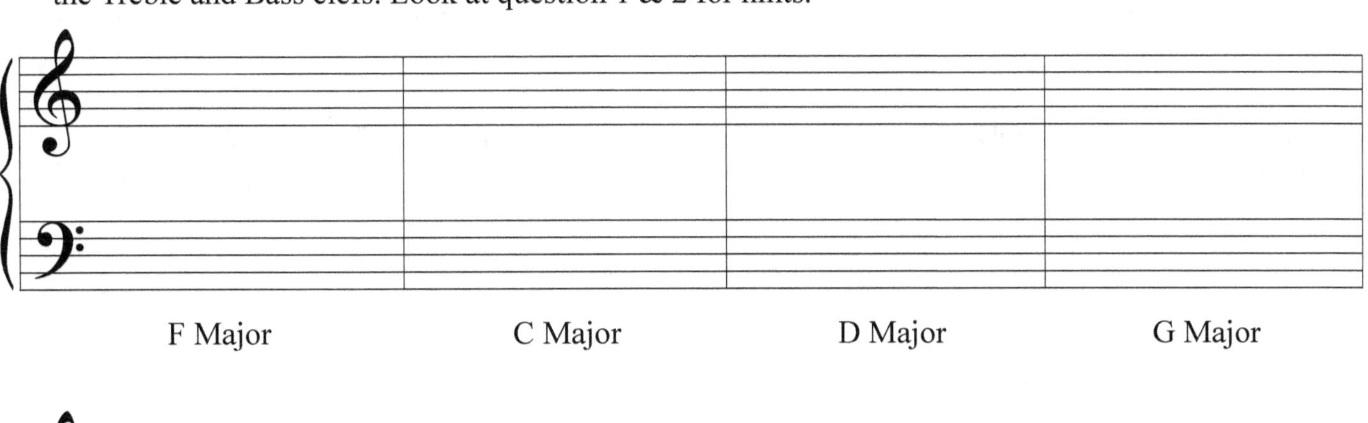

F Major C Major D Major G Major

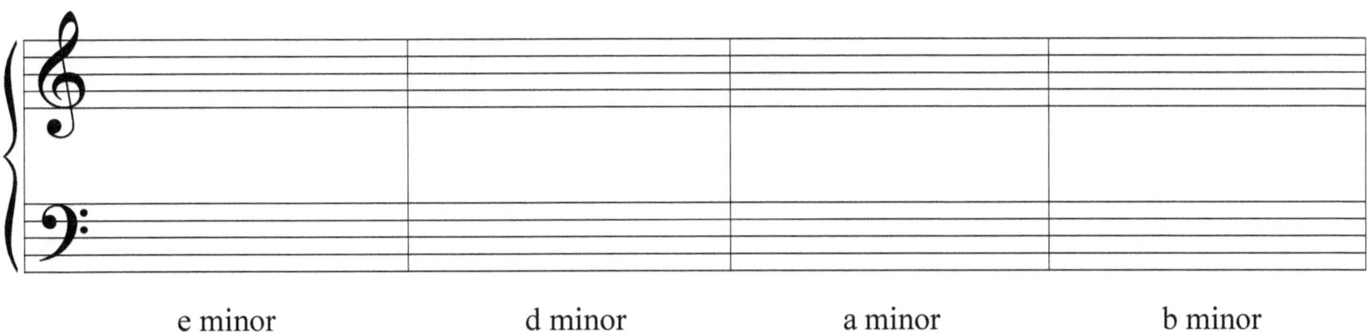

e minor d minor a minor b minor

4. Circle the three notes in the minor scales below that make up a root position triad.

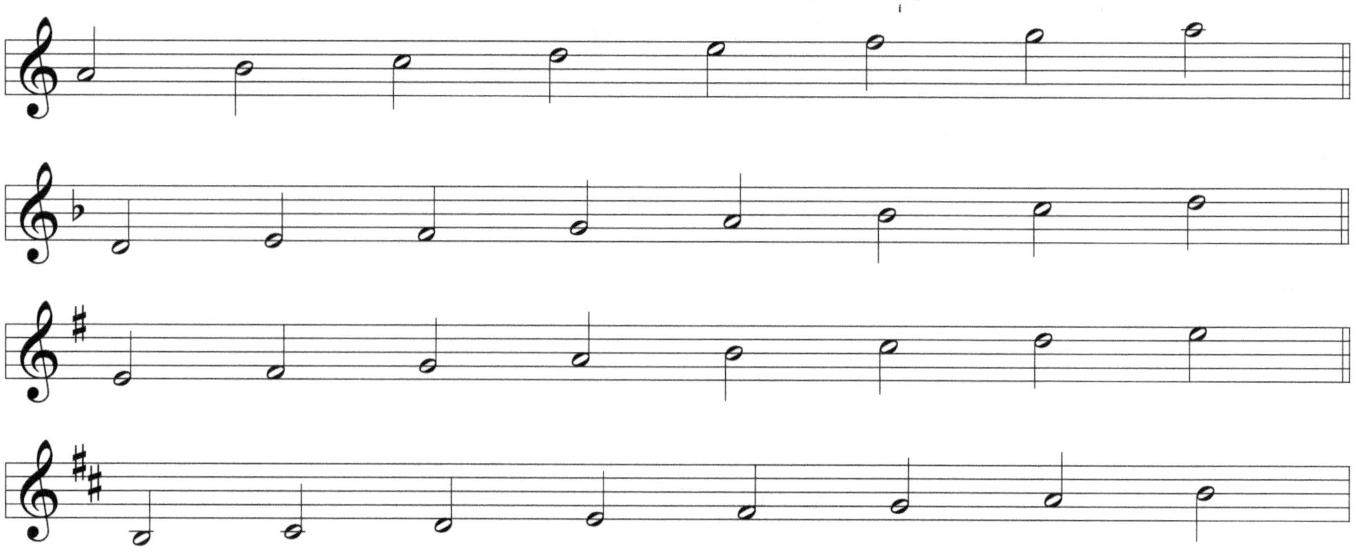

5. Each of these Major and minor triads should have 3 notes (Do-Mi-Sol/root-middle-top).
Fill in the missing note to create a root position triad for the given key.

Major keys

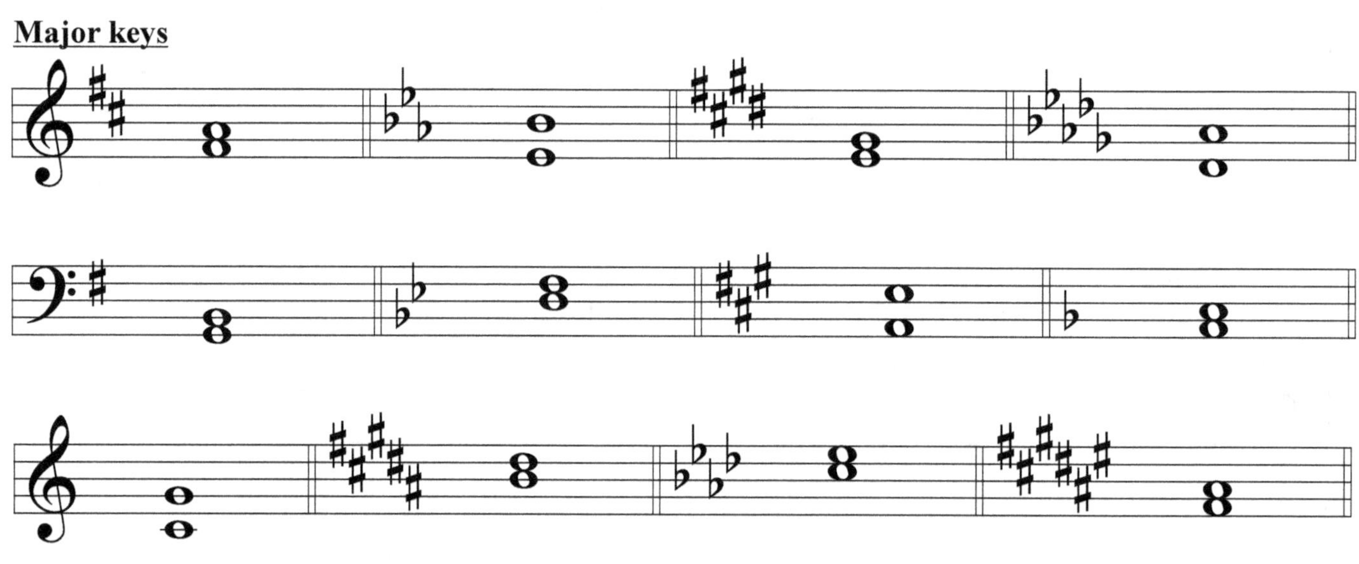

minor keys

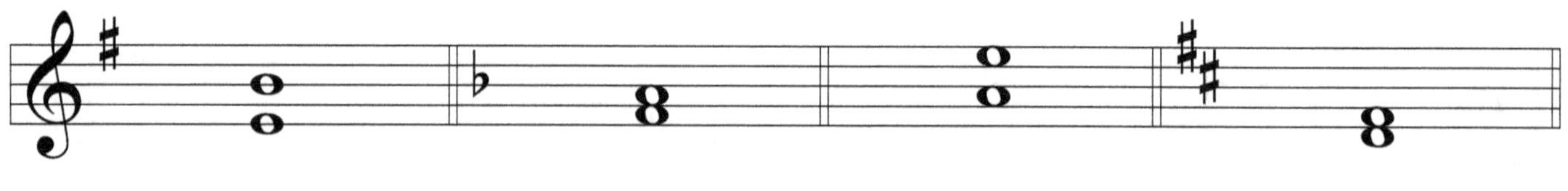

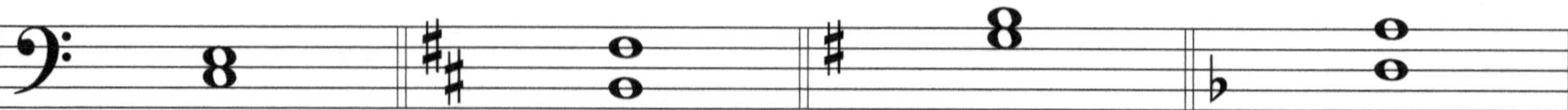

Review: Lessons 1-4

1. Name the note/rest and how many beats it has.

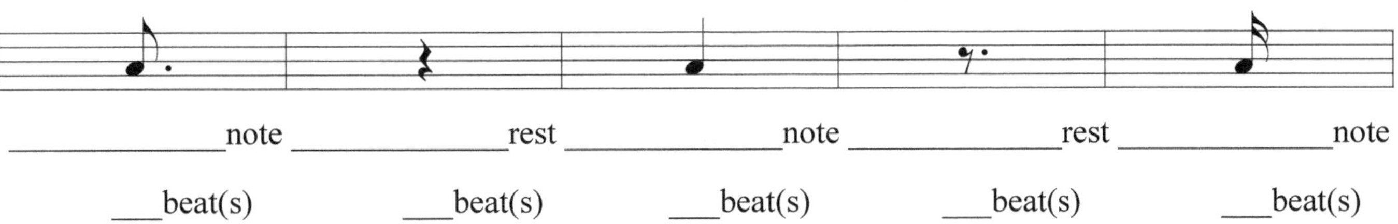

2. Check the correct counting for the example below.

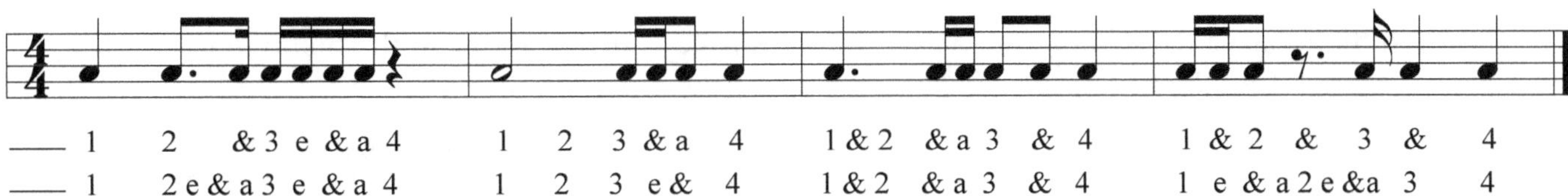

3. Write the beats under each note/rest in the following example.

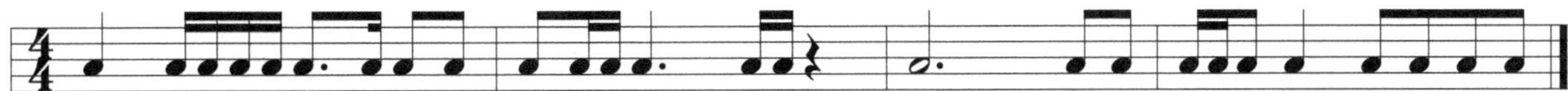

4. Add the 3 missing bar lines and a double bar line to the example below.

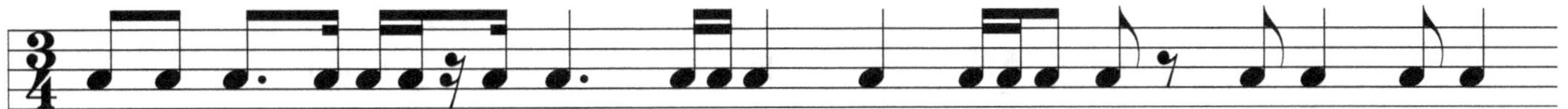

5. Add **one** missing note or rest to complete each measure in the example below.

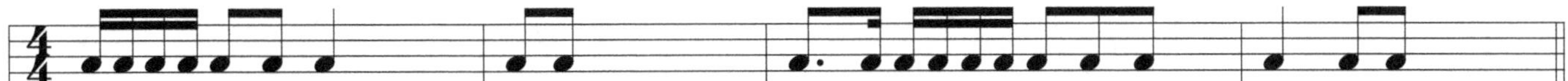

6. Check the Roman numeral for each triad in the following key.

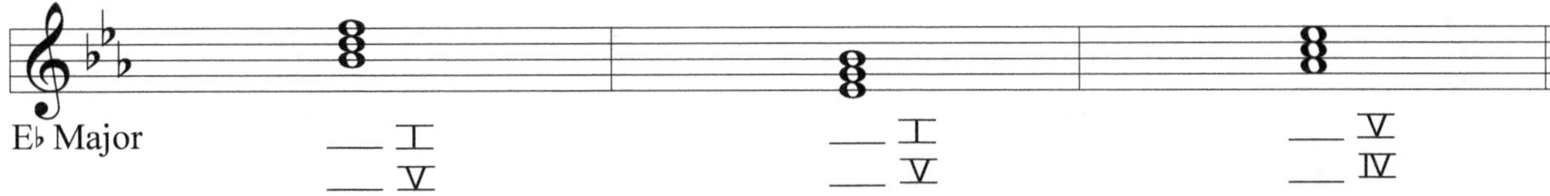

7. On the scale below:
   a. Add the Roman Numerals (I, IV, V) to the appropriate notes.
   b. Create a primary triad on the first, fourth, fifth & eighth notes of the scale.
   c. Add the necessary sharps according to the key that is given.

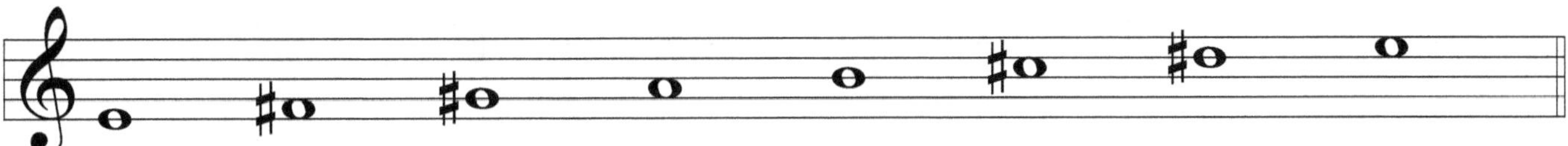

8. Write each Primary triad in the following key.

D♭ Major

I IV V

9. Circle the correct pattern of Whole steps and half steps that create a minor scale.

a. W H W W H W W

b. W W H W W W H

10. Fill in the relative minor key for each of the Major keys listed. Refer to the piano to count down 3 half steps to find the minor key, or go to the La of the scale.

G Major - ____minor C Major - ____minor

F Major - ____minor D Major - ____minor

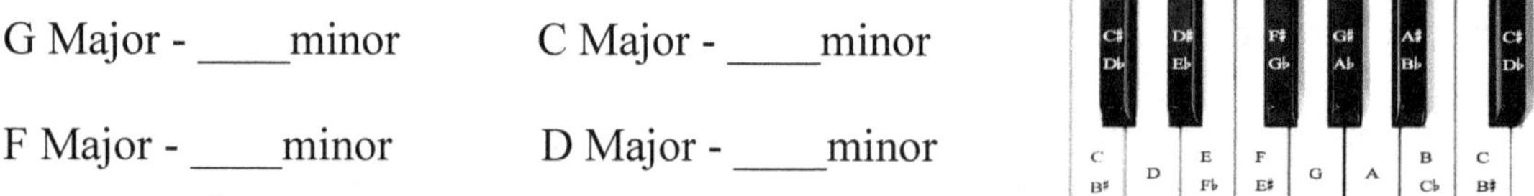

11. Name the following Major key signatures. Don't forget to add a ♯/♭ in the chord name, if necessary.

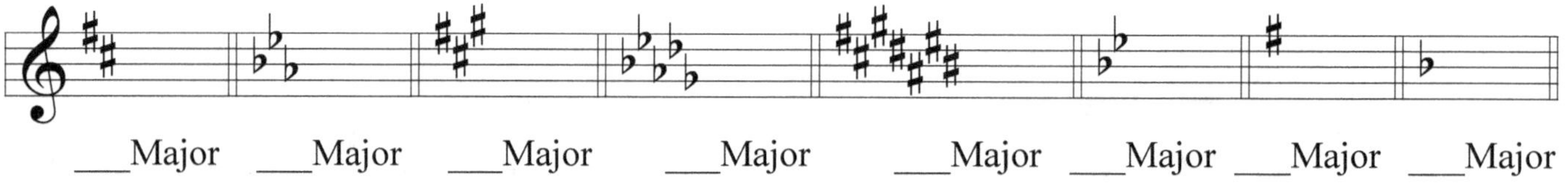

___Major ___Major ___Major ___Major ___Major ___Major ___Major ___Major

12. Name the minor key for each key signature.

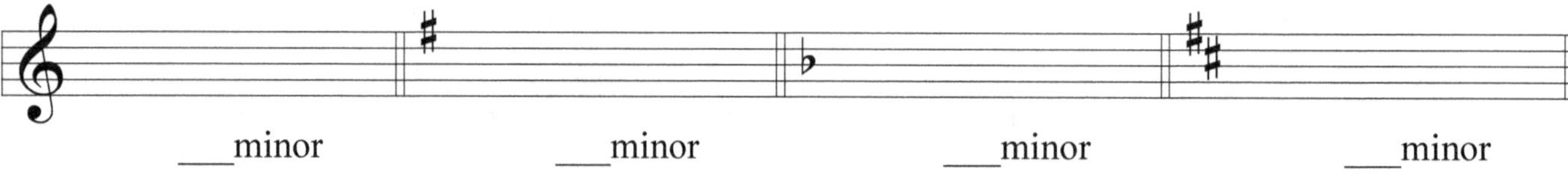

___minor ___minor ___minor ___minor

13. Draw the correct key signature, then add the root position triads for each minor key.

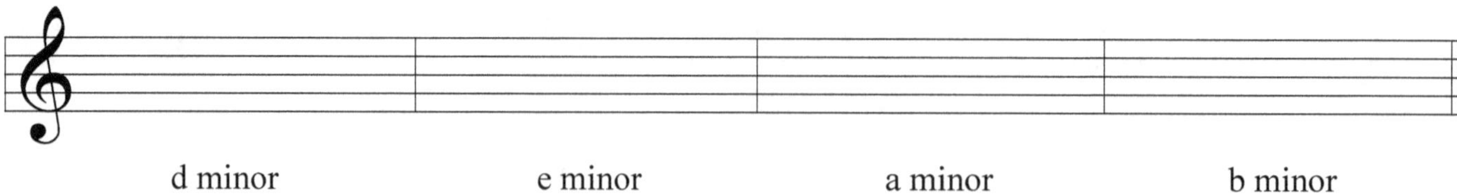

d minor e minor a minor b minor

14. Each of these minor triads should have 3 notes (Do-Mi-Sol/root-middle-top). Fill in the missing note to create a root position triad for the given minor keys.

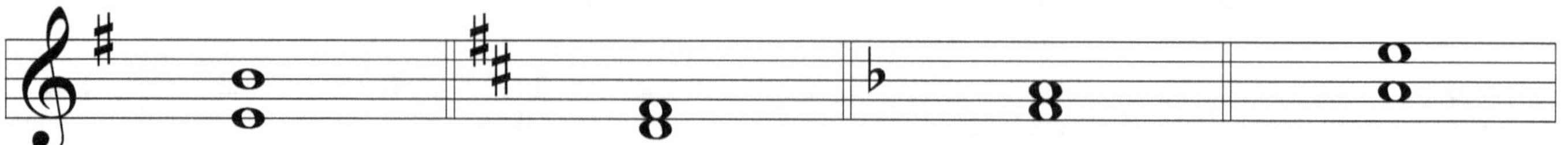

Lesson 5: Major and minor Intervals

An Interval in music, is the distance between any two notes. In this level, minor intervals will be introduced. We will review Major intervals and focus on minor 2nds, minor 3rds, minor 6ths & minor 7ths.

When counting intervals, be sure to include the bottom and top notes.

Minor intervals are closer together than Major intervals. In order to make an interval minor, you must either lower the top note or raise the bottom note. Look at the example below.

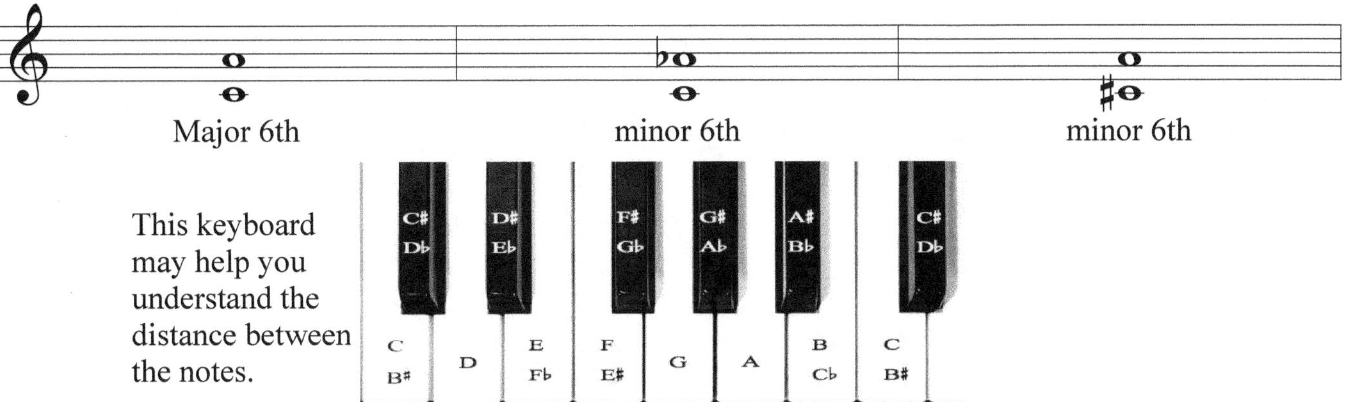

This keyboard may help you understand the distance between the notes.

All intervals in a Major scale are either Major or *Perfect. In the key of C Major for example:

C - D	C - E	C - F	C - G	C - A	C - B	C - C
Maj.2nd	Maj.3rd	Per. 4th	Per. 5th	Maj.6th	Maj.7th	Per.8th (Octave)

In order to determine whether an interval is Major or minor, you can consider the Major key signature of the bottom note. If the top note does not belong to the key, then the interval cannot be Major.

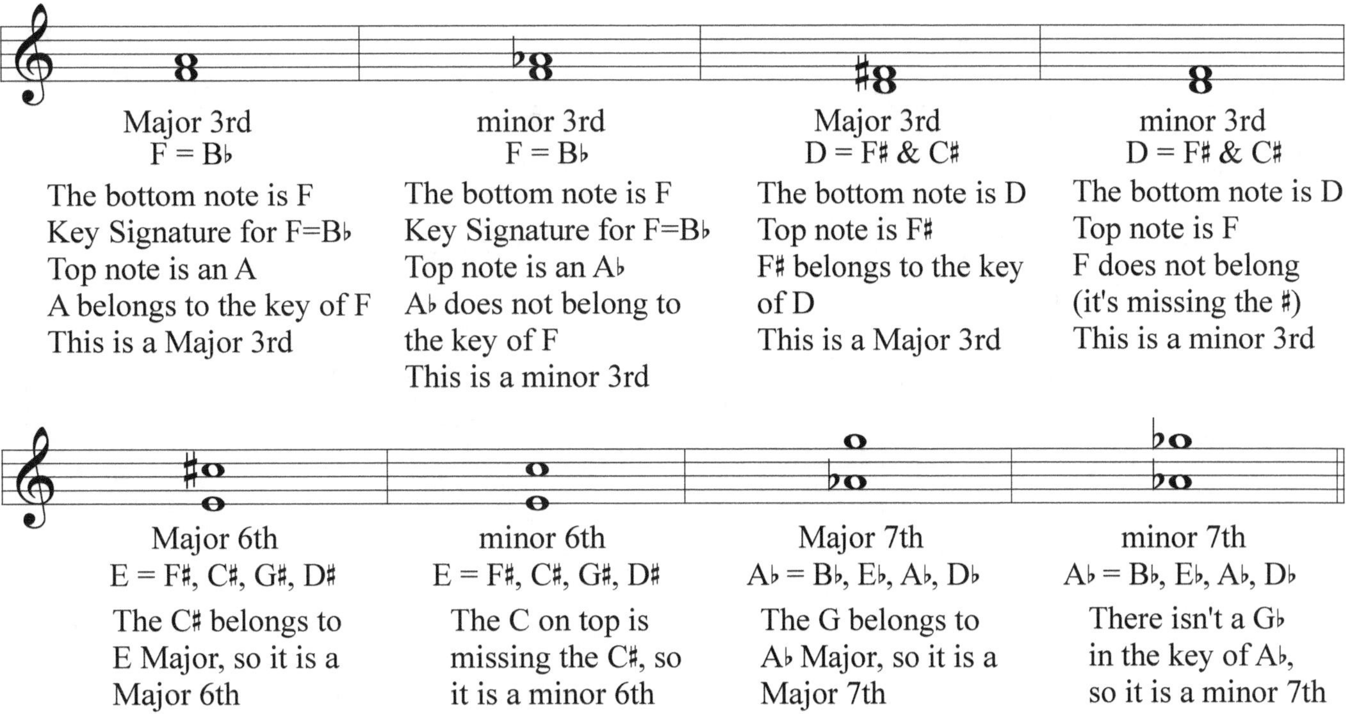

*4ths & 5ths can also be diminished or augmented. These will be covered in Level 6.

Below are more examples of melodic & harmonic minor 2nds, 3rds, 6ths & 7ths with the key signatures included. Flats or naturals were added to make the intervals minor.

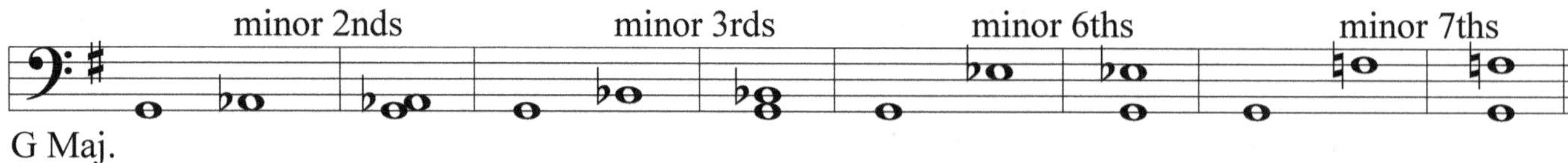

G Maj.

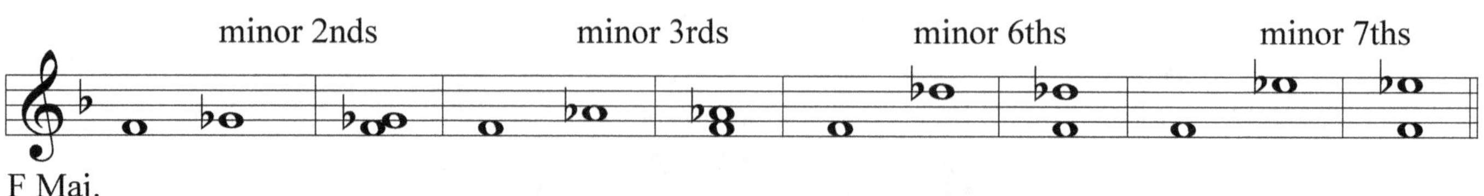

F Maj.

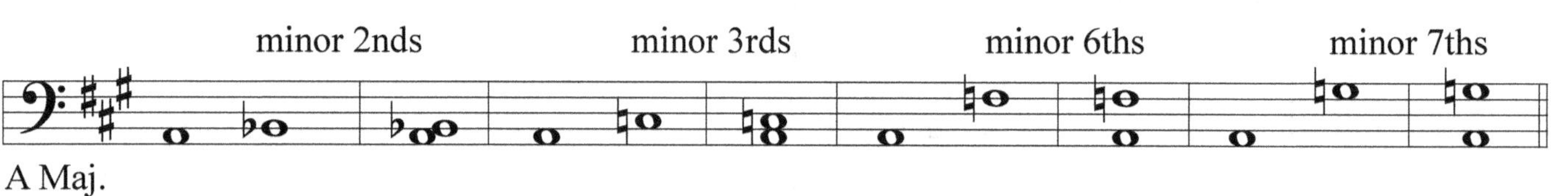

A Maj.

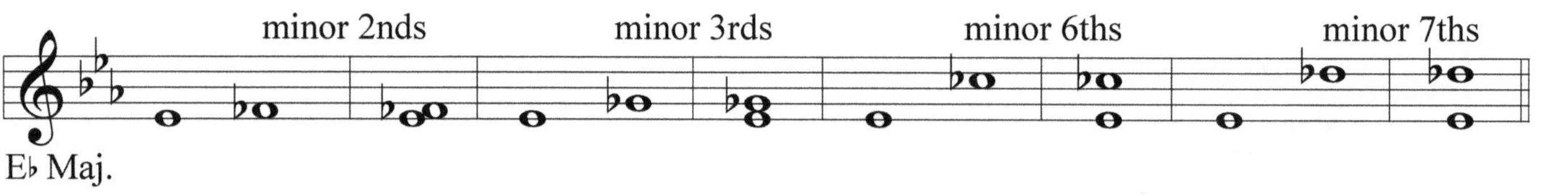

E♭ Maj.

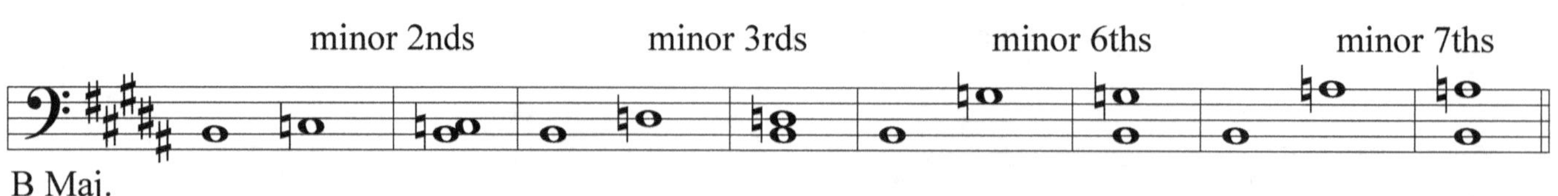

B Maj.

You can also learn how to identify Major and minor intervals by memorizing how many half or whole steps are between the two notes.

Interval	Distance between notes
minor 2nd	half step
Major 2nd	whole step
minor 3rd	1 1/2 steps
Major 3rd	2 (whole) steps
minor 6th	4 steps
Major 6th	4 1/2 steps
minor 7th	5 steps
Major 7th	5 1/2 steps

Here are the intervals in the key of C Major. Notice the distance in half steps & whole steps on the keyboard below.

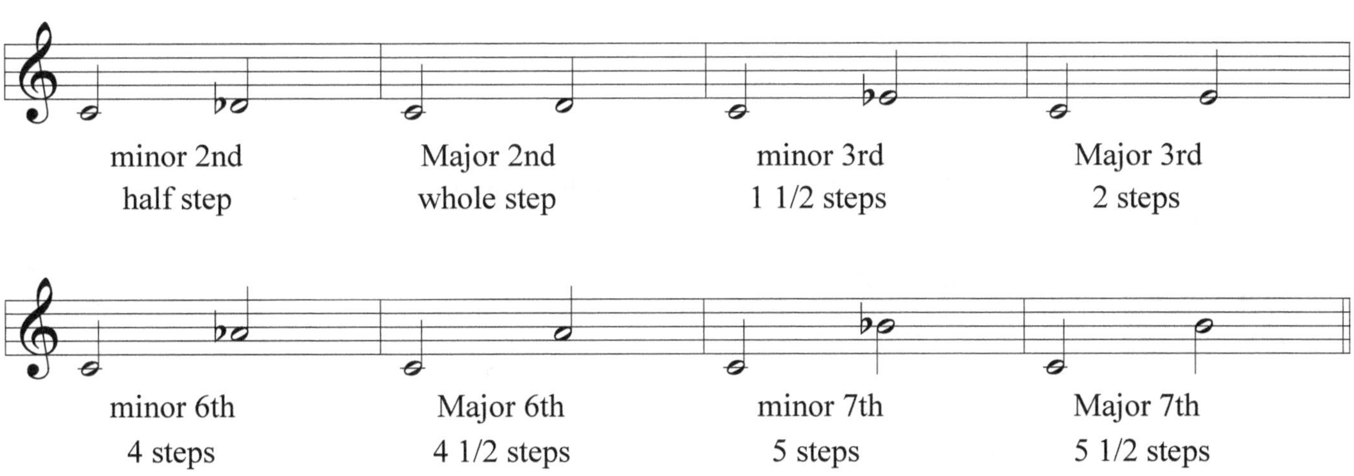

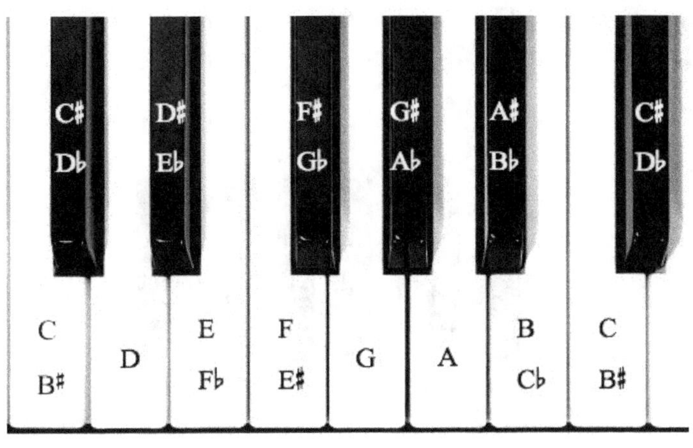

Review: Lesson 5

1. Label each interval. You may abbreviate Maj. and min. for Major and minor. Pay attention to the key signatures. The first one is done for you.

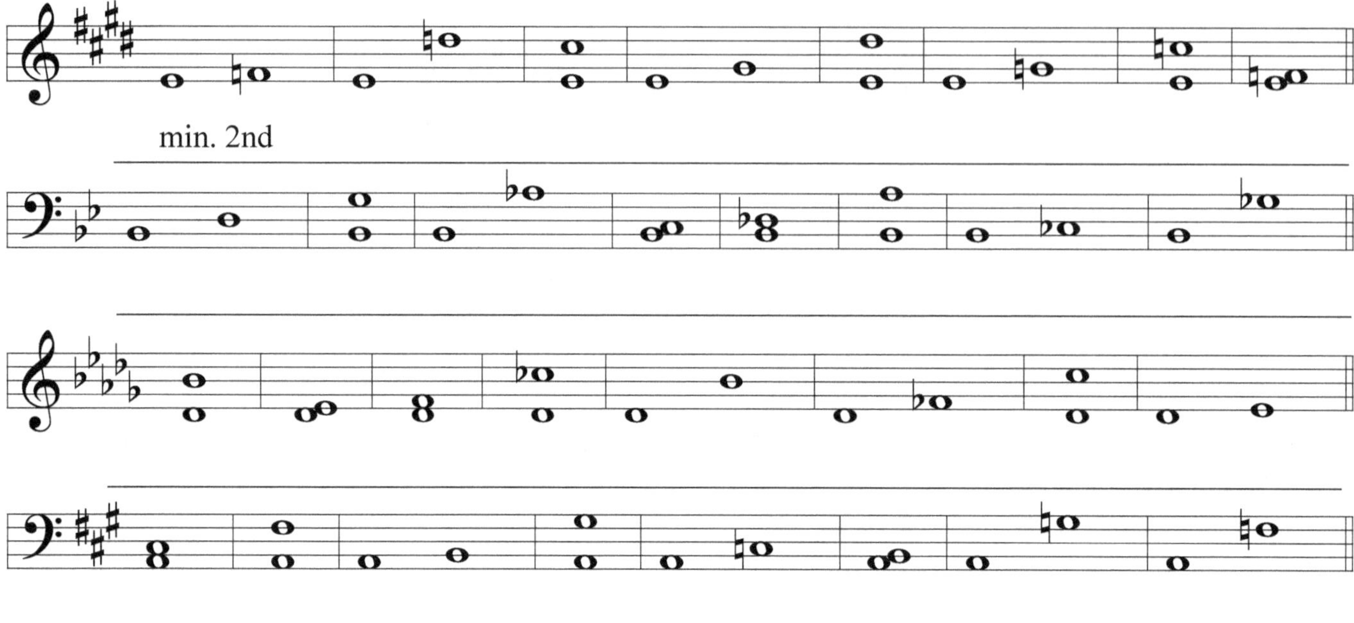

2. Check the correct name for each interval. M = Major, m = minor. Use the keyboard below for help. The first one is done for you.

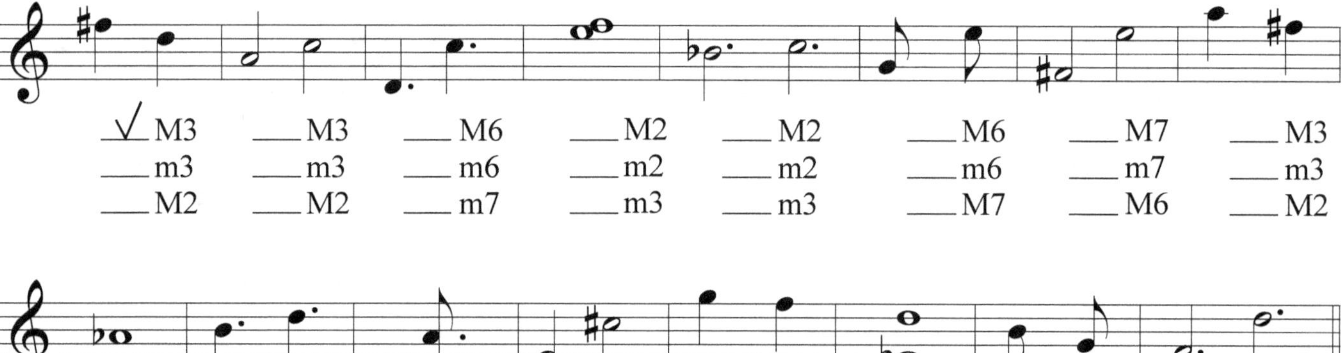

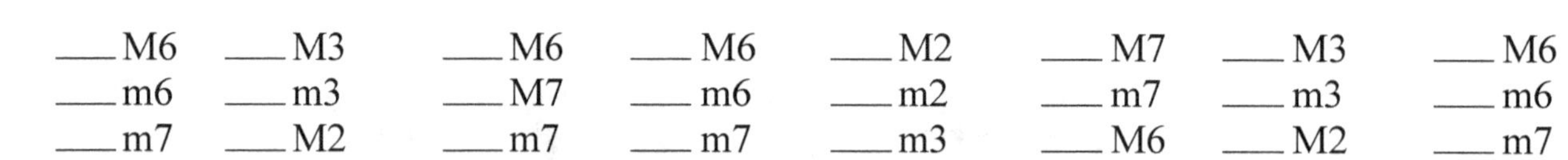

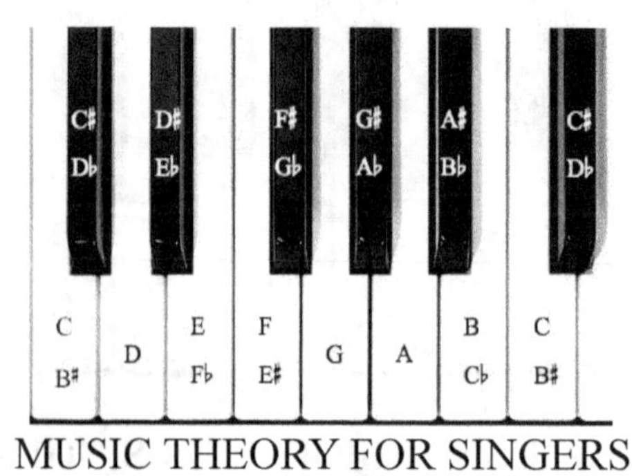

3. Write an H for half step or W for whole step under each measure. Remember that the natural half steps are between "mi-fa" and "ti-do." Pay attention to the key signatures. The first one is done for you.

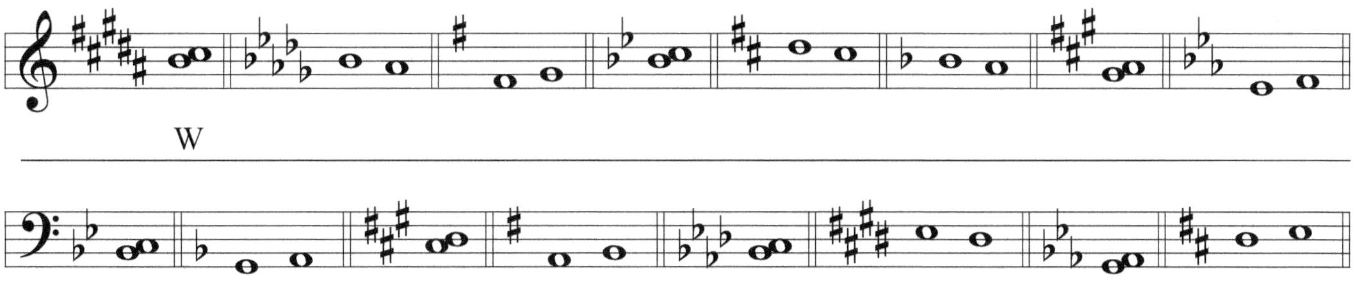

4. Circle all of the minor intervals. Remember to think of the Major key signature of the bottom note. If the top note does not belong to the key signature of the bottom note, then it's a minor interval. The first one is done for you.

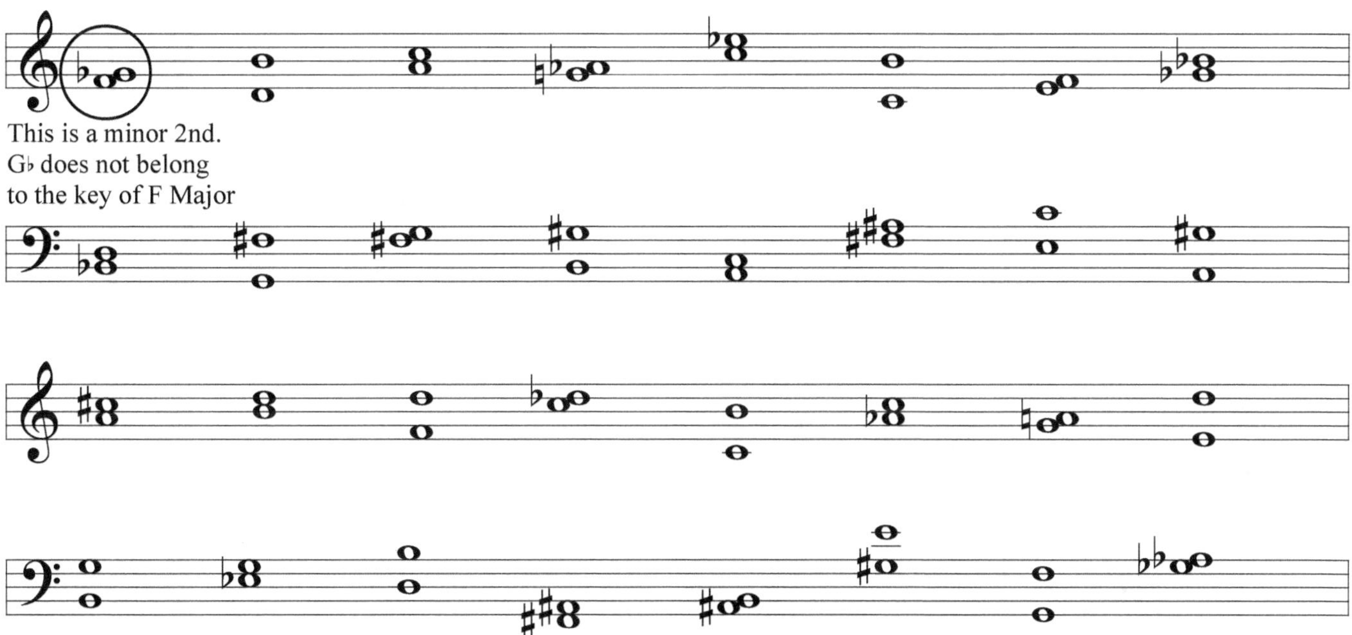

5. Add one note after and above the given note to complete the requested <u>melodic</u> interval. You may have to add an accidental. Use half notes. The first one is done for you.

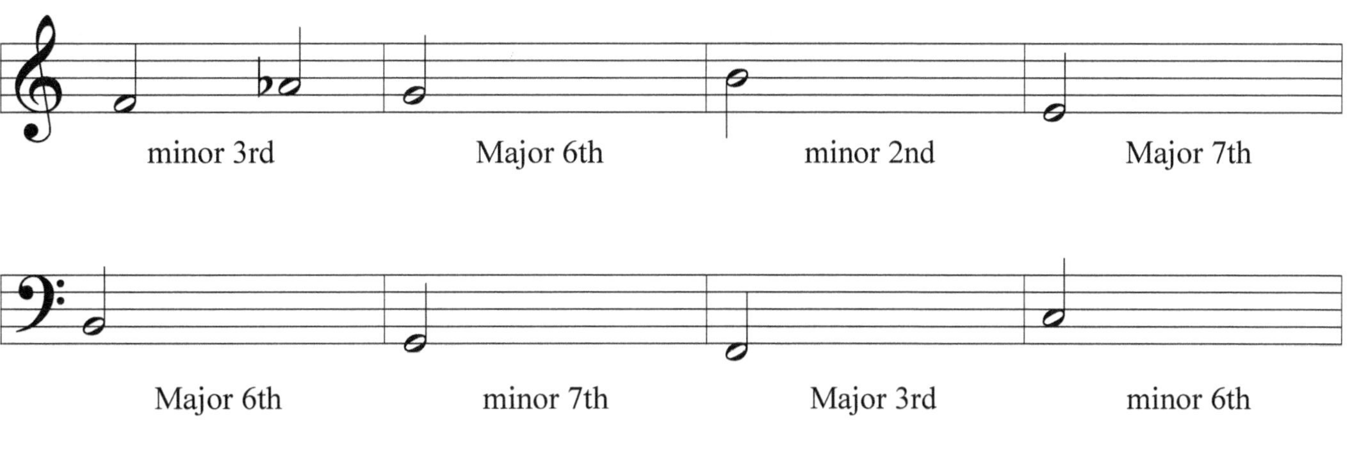

6. Add one note above the given note to complete the requested harmonic interval. You may have to add an accidental. Use whole notes. The first one is done for you.

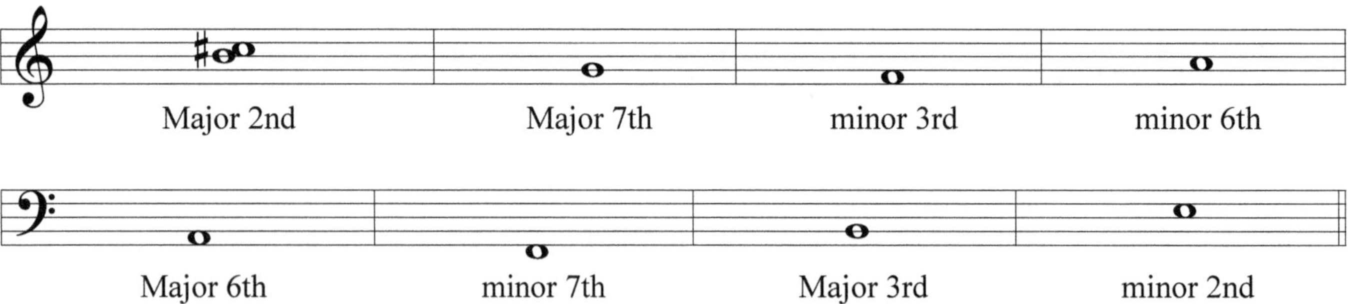

7. Add one note after and above the given note to create the requested melodic intervals. Pay attention to the key signatures. You may need to add sharp, flat or natural signs. Use quarter notes.

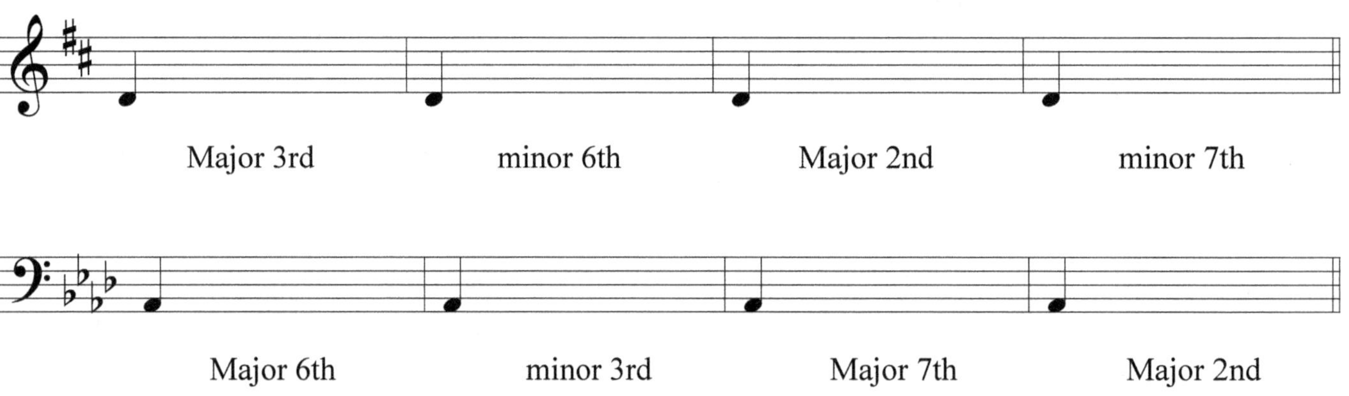

8. Add one note above the given note to create the requested harmonic intervals. Pay attention to the key signatures!

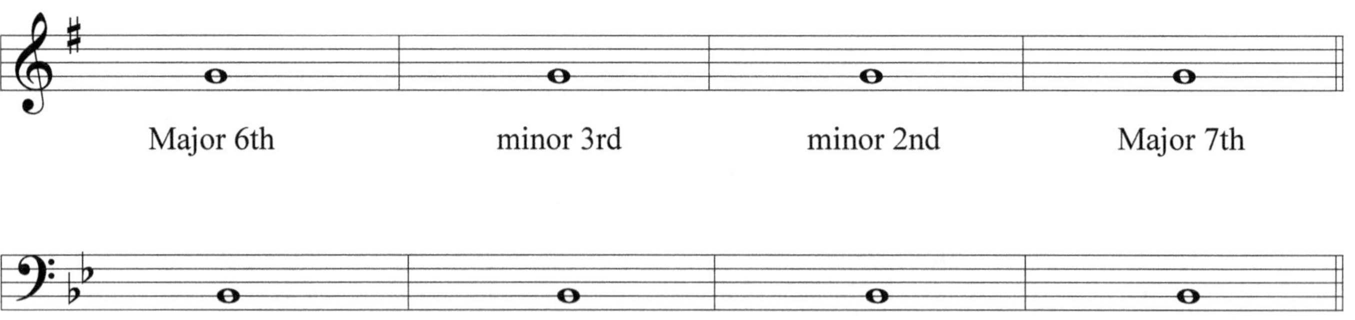

Lesson 6: Vocal Diction & IPA

Every time we sing a song, we are telling a story. As singers, we have to be exceptionally clear with how we pronounce the words of our songs, or our audience will not understand us and our story will not be told.

If you reference a dictionary in any Latin based language (English, Italian, French, German, Spanish, Latin, etc.) you will see some symbols next to the words. These symbols make up the International Phonetic Alphabet, or IPA. The IPA represents the sounds of a language. In fact, the IPA represents nearly any vowel or consonant made by human beings!

In this lesson, we'll focus on a few of the sounds in the IPA. You will learn what the letter looks like in our language, what the IPA symbol for that letter is, and what it sounds like. The IPA symbols from Levels 1-4 will also be in a chart on the following page.

Before we look at the symbols, make a couple of sounds so you can see all of the different positions your tongue moves to in order to make each sound.

Say "ah" as in the word "father," and "ee" as in the word "meet." You'll notice that when you say "ah," your tongue is at the bottom of your mouth, and when you say "ee" the center of your tongue moves to the roof of your mouth, while the tip remains down and behind the bottom teeth. When singing, we must be aware of any tension in our tongue, and ensure that it is in the proper position for creating accurate vowel sounds.

Here is a chart of the consonants we will learn in this lesson, along with their english equivalent.

ɲ	canyon	[kaɲjon]	High tongue Tip touching hard palate Lips relaxed
h	ham	[hæm]	Low, flat tongue Open, wide mouth Lips relaxed
ŋ	sing	[siŋg]	High tongue Middle touching soft palate Lips relaxed
ð	this	[ðɪs]	Mid tongue Tip between teeth Lips relaxed

Courtesy of Sarah Sandvig

Practice saying the sounds above, and the english words in the second column.

Check that your tongue and lips are in the position described in the last column.

Additional IPA symbols, like the ones you see in the 3rd column will be introduced in later levels of these books.

Below is a chart of the vowels introduced in Levels 1, 2, & 3.

Practice looking at each symbol, then say the english word and pay attention to the tongue and lips position described in the third column.

IPA SYMBOL	SOUND IN ENGLISH WORD	IPA SPELLING OF WORD	TONGUE/LIPS PLACEMENT
i	ski	[ski]	Center of tongue is high Lips relaxed
ɛ	led	[lɛd]	Low tongue Lips relaxed
ɑ	father	[ˈfɑðər]	Low tongue Lips relaxed
o	obey	[oʊˈbeɪ]	Low tongue, tip behind bottom teeth Rounded lips
u	goose	[gus]	Low tongue, tip behind bottom teeth Rounded lips
ɪ	kit	[kɪt]	High tongue, sides touching top teeth Lips relaxed
e	ate	[eɪt]	High tongue, sides touching top teeth Lips relaxed
ə	afraid	[əˈfreɪd]	Mid tongue, tip behind bottom teeth Lips relaxed
æ	cat	[kæt]	Mid tongue, tip behind bottom teeth Lips slightly horizontal
ʊ	book	[bʊk]	Low tongue, tip below bottom teeth Lips relaxed
ʌ	strut	[strʌt]	Low tongue, tip behind bottom teeth Lips relaxed
ɔ	forest	[fɔrəst]	Low tongue, tip behind bottom teeth Lips slightly rounded

Courtesy of Sarah Sandvig

Note: The schwa (ə) and the "uh" vowel (ʌ) are very similar. The schwa (ə) is unaccented and not stressed, while the (ʌ) is open and emphasized, like in the words "money or "under."

Below is a chart of the vowels and consonants introduced in Level 4 followed by the new IPA symbols for this level.

Practice looking at each symbol, then say the english word and pay attention to the tongue and lips position described in the third column.

oʊ (diphthong: 2 vowel sounds)	goat	[goʊt]	Low tongue, tip behind bottom teeth Lips open then rounded
aɪ (diphthong: 2 vowel sounds)	price	[praɪs]	Low tongue then high tongue tip behind bottom teeth then sides touching top teeth Lips tall then relaxed
ʤ	jar	[ʤɑr]	High tongue on hard palate tip behind top teeth Lips rounded
j	yet	[jɛt]	High tongue sides touching top teeth tip behind bottom teeth Lips relaxed
ʃ	ship	[ʃɪp]	High tongue sides touching top teeth Lips rounded
ɲ	canyon	[kaɲon]	High tongue Tip touching hard palate Lips relaxed
h	ham	[hæm]	Low, flat tongue Open, wide mouth Lips relaxed
ŋ	sing	[siŋg]	High tongue Middle touching soft palate Lips relaxed
ð	this	[ðɪs]	Mid tongue Tip between teeth Lips relaxed

Courtesy of Sarah Sandvig

Review: Lesson 6

1. Check the English word that contains the same sound as the given IPA symbol.

ɲ	___Onion ___Banner	j	___Just ___Yet	u	___Goose ___Put	ɑ	___Bother ___Pat
h	___Exit ___Hot	ʤ	___Just ___Danger	aɪ	___Mate ___Rice	ʊ	___But ___Nook
ð	___Then ___Orange	oʊ	___Goat ___Ouch	o	___Rope ___Bought	ɔ	___Jot ___Boat
ŋ	___Ring ___Naughty	ʌ	___Loop ___Mutt	e	___Pay ___Get	ɛ	___Beet ___Let
ʃ	___Shine ___Soon	æ	___Apple ___Ate	ɪ	___Right ___Fit	ə	___Amazing ___Fate
i	___Bit ___Fleet						

2. Write a word in the blank provided that uses the given IPA sound. Don't use any of the words from above or on the previous pages!

e __________________	aɪ __________________	ʌ __________________
ɪ __________________	oʊ __________________	ʊ __________________
u __________________	a __________________	æ __________________
o __________________	ɔ __________________	ə __________________
i __________________	ɑ __________________	ŋ __________________
j __________________	ʤ __________________	ʃ __________________
h __________________	ð __________________	ɲ __________________

Lesson 7: Italian, Latin & Spanish Diction

When you first learn a song in a foreign language, Italian and Latin are two of the easier languages to pronounce. Below are some rules for speaking/singing words in Italian and Latin that can help you learn how to prounounce the text in your songs.

It's also a great idea to use a translation app or website to hear someone pronounce the foreign language text as well.

Italian/Latin Diction

As with any language, practicing speaking this language with an Italian accent will help with pronunciation. IPA is included in parentheses after each Italian/Latin word.

Remember: No diphthongs!
•*Core* (kore) is pronounced Core-A, but without the E sound at the end of A.
Another example is *Mio* (mˈio) is pronounced Mee-oh but without the oo sound and the end of O.

•I's are pronounced like E's. (ie) *Ma'mi* (mami) is pronounced Mamee

•All R's are rolled or flipped. If you cannot roll your R's, try something similar to a D. *Caro* (karo) would sound similar to *Cah-doh*, then add a little less pressure to the roof of your mouth. Your tongue touches the top of your hard palate behind your top front teeth for the first letter.
**Two great practice exercises to learn how to roll your tongue is to say "Podda tea" over and over again, or try saying"Tah-dah" over and over again.

•A "C" followed by an E or I is pronounced as a "CH." (ie) *Facil* (fatʃil) is pronounced Facheel.
Also *Dolce* (doltʃe) is pronounced Dole-cheh.
•A "CH" combo is pronounced as a K. (ie) *Chiaro* (kjaro) is pronounced Kee-ah-ro.

•When a word has a double consonant, you stop on the first consonant then continue. The best example of this is the word "*Pizza*" (piddza). It's not pronounced PEEZA, it's pronounced PEETSA.
Also *Quella* (kwella) is Kwell-lah.

•A "G" if it's before an e or an i is a soft g. (ie) *gentil* (dʒentil) is pronounced jenteel, *Giardi* (dʒardi) is pronounced Jar-dee. Notice the "i" is silent when it falls between G and another vowel. The same rule applies when an "i" falls between C and another vowel as in "*ciao.*" ch-ow
•A "G" followed by an "L" is silent. (ie) *scegliera* (ʃeʎʎera) is pronounced shay-lee-err-ah.
•A G followed by an H is pronounced as a Hard G...*Lunghezza* (luŋgettsa) is pronounced Loon-get-tsa.

•*Que* (kwe) is pronounced Kway.
•*Che* (ke) is pronounced Kay.

•An S followed by a C is pronounced as an SH. (ie) *s'angoscia* (ssaŋgoʃʃa) is san-go-shah.
•If an S is followed by a CH it's pronounced as SK. (ie) *scherzosa* (skertsoza) is scare-tso-za.
•A single S between two vowels is pronounced as a Z. (ie) *ascosa* (askoza) is pronounced ah-sko-za.
•An SC before e or i is pronounced as an SH. (ie) *scegliera* (ʃeʎʎera) is pronounced shay-lee-err-ah.

•An H at the beginning of a word is silent. (ie) *Hanno* (anno) is pronounced Ahn-no.

•A Z is pronounced like TS. (ie) *Danza* (dantsa) is pronounced Dawn-tsa.

•An "A" is pronounced as an "AH"

Spanish Diction

When singing in Spanish, pay special attention to where the composer is from. Spanish pronunciation differs slightly depending on the country. It's always best to listen to a recording, if possible, of a singer or speaker who is from the same country as the composer.

Remember: No diphthongs!

Noche is pronounced No-chay, but without the E sound at the end of A.

Another example is *Mio* is pronounced Mee-oh but without the oo sound and the end of O.

•Roll all R's that begin a word.
•Flip all R's at the end of a word.
•Roll or flip all R's in the middle of a word depending on how it is usually pronounced.

•The "C" sound is different in Spanish from Spain as opposed to Spanish from Mexico and other countries. The Spain "C" is pronounced with a th sound like a lisp (ie) *hacer* is pronounced Hather. In Mexico, it's just an "S" sound (ie) *hacer* is pronounced Ha-ser.

•Double LL's are pronounced as a Y. (ie) *Llega* is pronounced Yeah-gah.

•T's and D's use a flatter tongue, more dentalized. These two consonants are not as bright as we say them in English. Example: *todos* is toe-those, and **not** toe-dohs.

•Pay special attention to accents, and pronounce them as spoken.

•Pronounce J's with a small puff of air, in order for it to be audible, similar to an H. (ie) *Reja* is pronounced Ray-ha.

•Always hold the first vowel when singing a word with a diphthong.

•*Que* is pronounced as Kay.
•*Che* is pronounced as Chay.

•An ñ is pronounced as in the word Ke**nya**.

•A Y (the letter that stands for the word "and") is pronounced as an E, as in "key."

•E's are pronounced as the IPA symbol "e" as in "Pay" when in the middle of a word.
•E's are pronounced as the IPA symbol "ɛ" as in "let" when at the beginning of a word.

•I's are pronounced as E's. *Mi* is pronounced as Mee.

•G followed by an i or e is pronounced with the H sound like *gente* hente or *Ginastera* Hinastera.
•G followed by a u is a hard G as in *gusta* goos-tah

Review: Lesson 7

1. Circle "True" or "False" for the following questions about **Spanish** pronunciation.

J's are pronounced like an H.

True False

I's are pronounced as in the word "eye."

True False

"Che" is pronounced as Kay.

True False

2. For the following questions, check the correct choice that best describes how the Italian, Latin, or Spanish words would be pronounced.

Spanish

Niña	___Neenya ___Neena	Dio	___Dee-oh ___Dye-oh	Pollo	___Pah-low ___Poy-yo
Ojos	___Oh-Johs ___Oh-hohs	Y	___Why ___EE	Hora	___Hore-ah ___Oh-rah
Cuestra	___Kwestrah ___Kestrah	Esto	___Es-toh ___Ease-toh	Triste	___Tree-stay ___Trist-ee
Tengo	___Ten-Go ___Tang-Go	Fuera	___Fwhere-ah ___Foo-rah	Llega	___Yay-gah ___Lay-gah
Que	___Kay ___Kway	Majo	___Mah-joh ___Mah-ho	Gigante	___Jee-gone-teh ___Hee-gone-tay

Italian/Latin

Lascia	___La-Shah ___La-Skee-Ah	Tuba	___Too-bah ___Tub-bah	Respiro	___Ress-peer-oh ___Rees-pie-roh
Ancora	___Ann-core-ah ___Awn-core-ah	Cara	___Cay-rah ___Cah-rah	Dona	___Dawn-ah ___Doan-ah
Quartetto	___Kwartet-toh ___Kartetto	Cessa	___Sess-ah ___Chess-ah	Giorni	___Jor-nee ___Gye-or-nye
Orchestra	___Or-chest-trah ___Or-kes-tra	Di	___Dye ___Dee	Piace	___Pee-ah-chay ___Pie-ah-say

Lesson 8: Sight-Singing

In order to learn a song, singers learn to read both rhythmic patterns and notes (melody) on the staff. Singing a melody for the first time is called "sight-singing." Below are some rhythmic examples using the notes introduced so far.

Hint: When singing rhythmic examples, take a breath on the rests: then you won't miss them! *Tap* and *say* the beats, then sing the examples on La (choose any pitch that suits your voice).

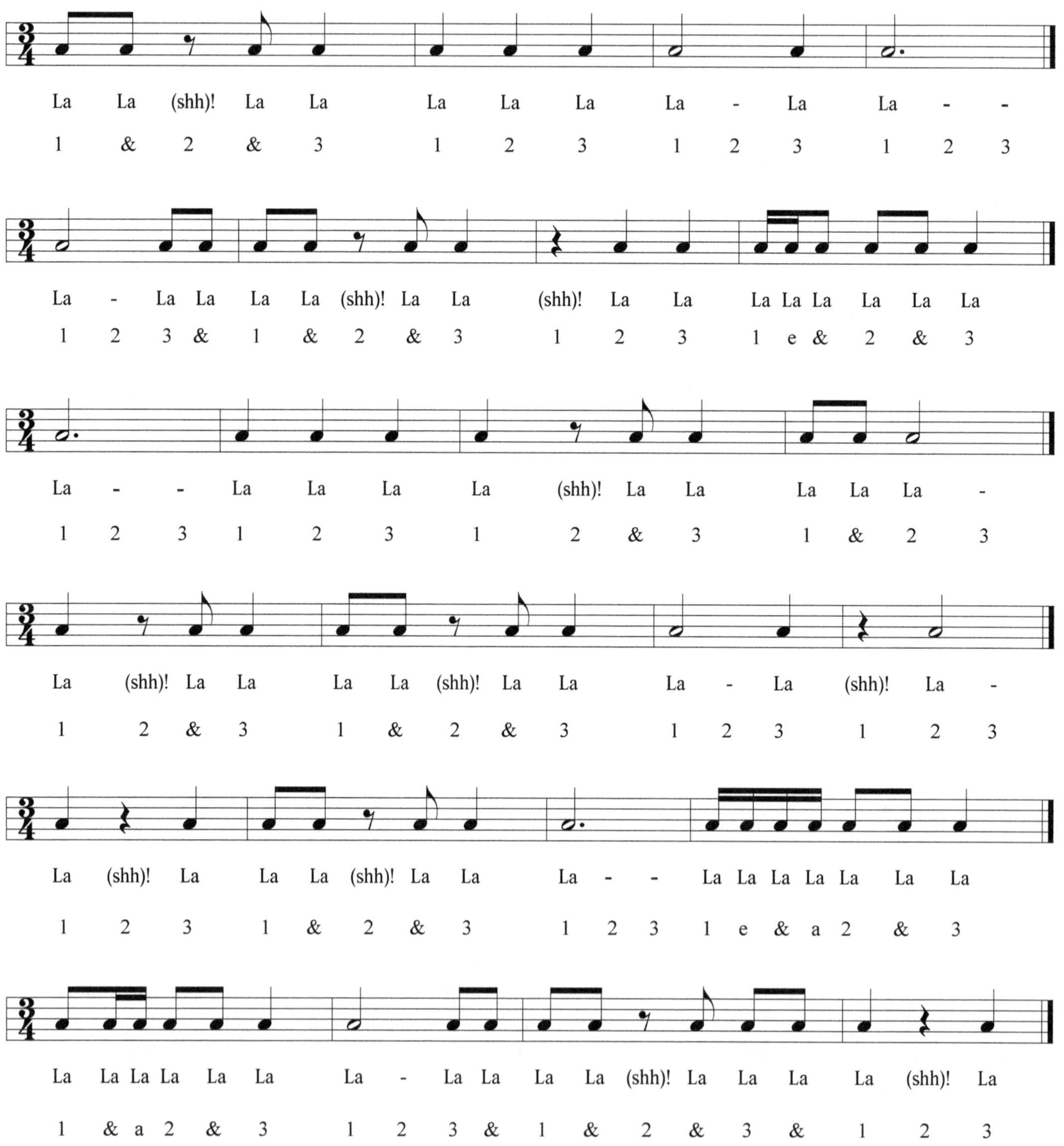

Melody & Solfege

Solfege is a system of assigning a syllable to each note of a scale, just like in the song "Do-Re-Mi" from the musical *The Sound of Music.*

Solfege is a useful tool when sight-singing. Moveable "Do" is when "Do" matches the **root** of whatever key you're in.

In this Level, you'll learn to sing melodies with Do, Re, Mi, Fa, Sol, La & Ti. The following melodies have the solfege written under the notes for you. Pay attention to the key signature changes. Use the picture of the piano below to find your starting note on your piano or piano app.

Here are some examples in F & E Major (high voices), and D♭ & C Major (lower voices).

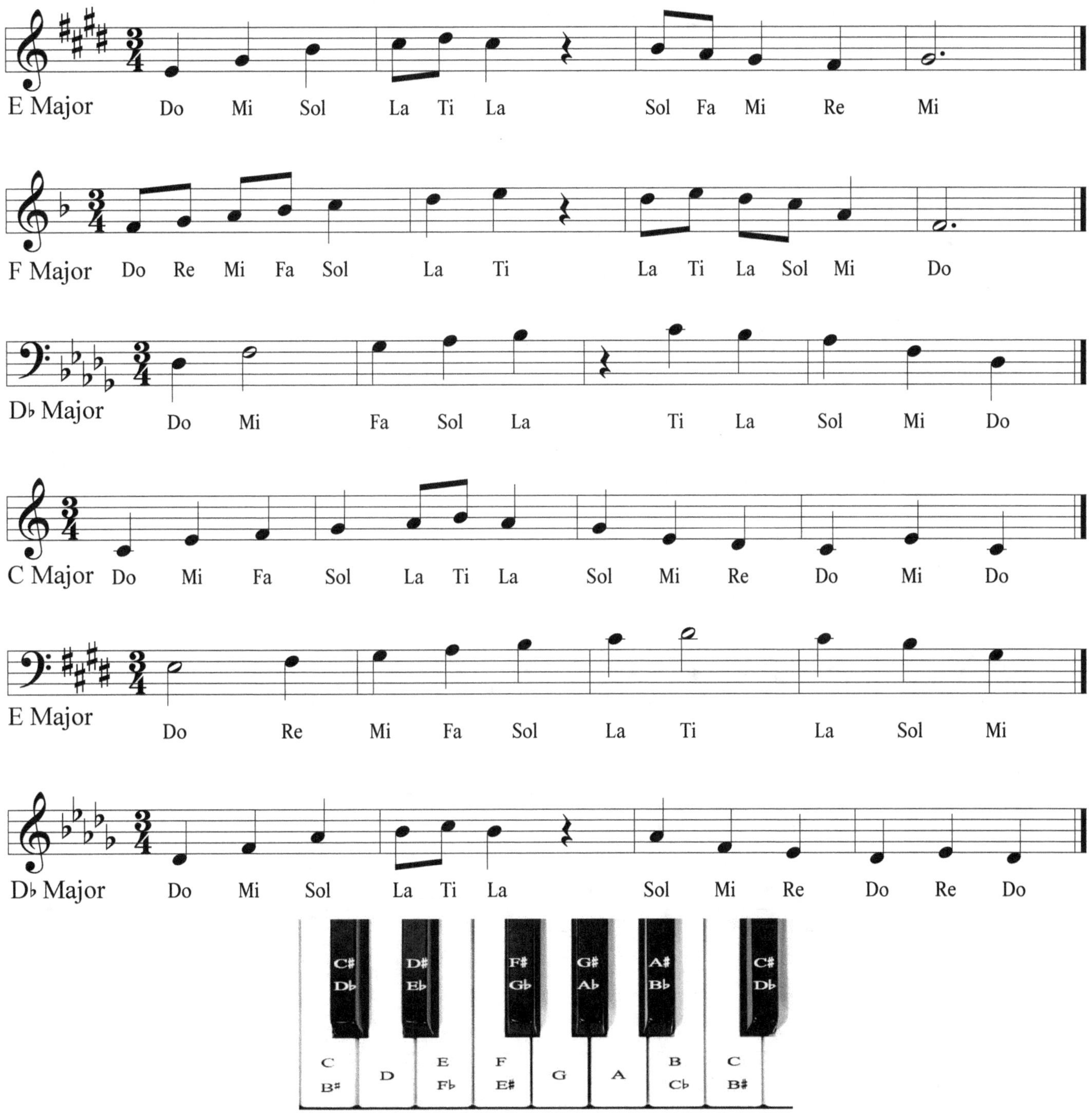

Review: Lesson 8

1. For the following melodies, write the note names, solfege & beats underneath the notes.
   Practice singing the examples when you are done!

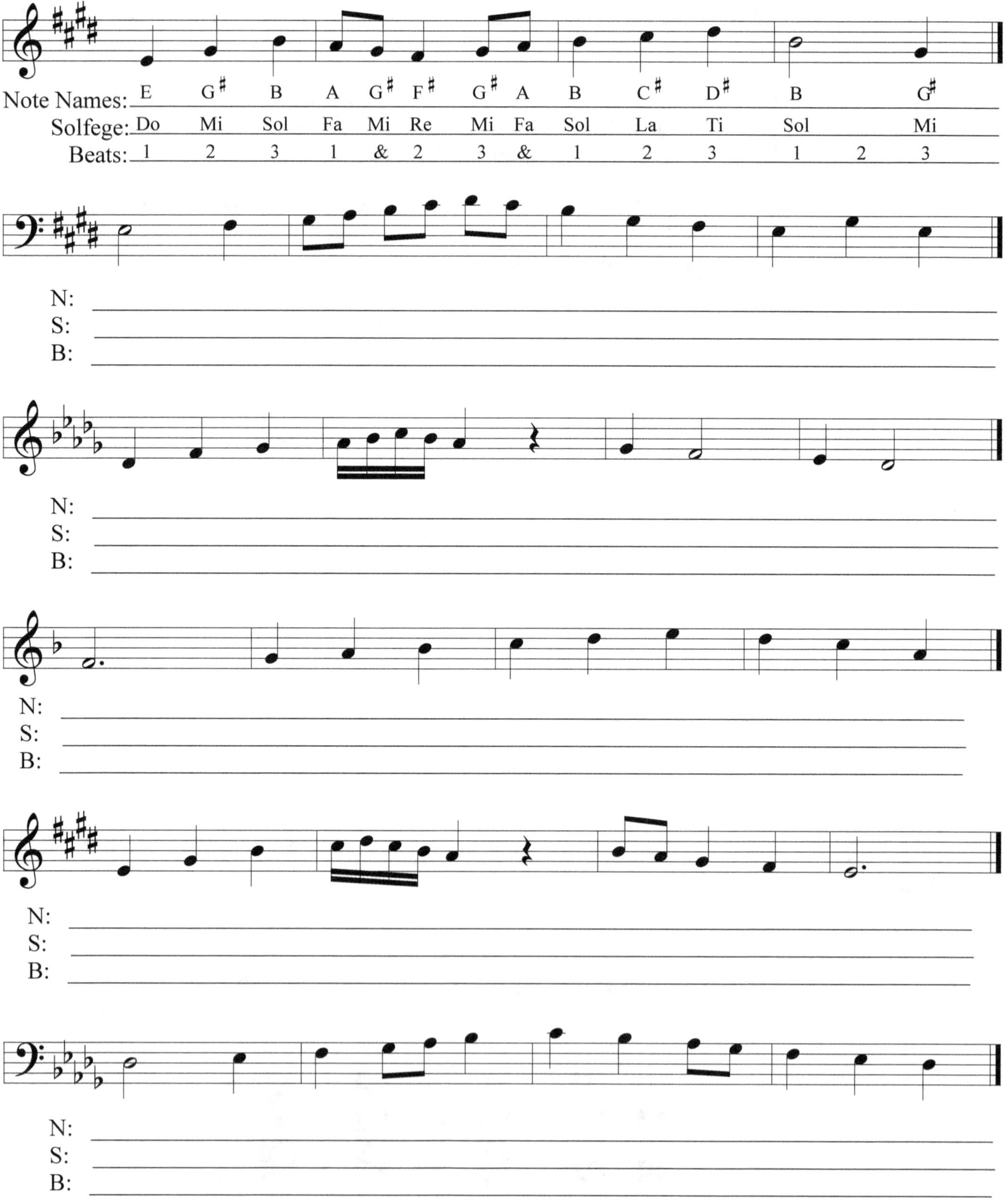

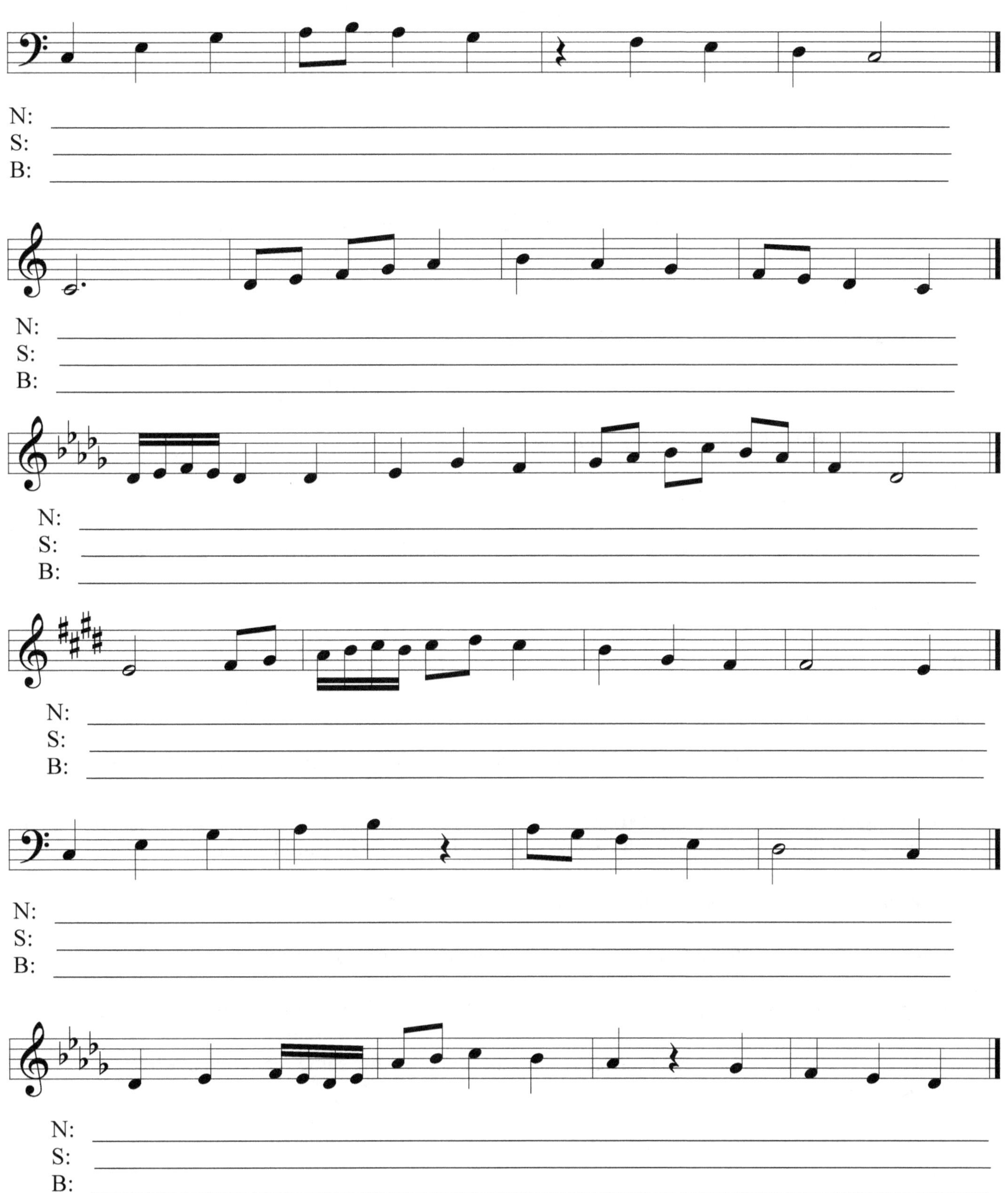
N:
S:
B:
N:
S:
B:
N:
S:
B:
N:
S:
B:
N:
S:
B:
N:
S:
B:

Lesson 9: Musical Terms

A crucial part of understanding music is being able to recognize and define musical terms. Below is a list of terms covered in this level.

alla breve / cut time (𝄵) - the same as 2 / 2 time

arietta - a short aria

bel canto - brilliant, lyric vocal style originating in Italy in the 18th & early 19th centuries

coda - a separate section at the end of a song, usually indicated by the symbol (𝄌)

common time (𝄴) - the same as 4 / 4 time

da capo (D.C.) - return to the beginning

da capo aria - a vocal form popular in the Baroque era, with an ABA form

D.C. al fine - return to the beginning and sing to the fine

dal segno (D.S.) - return to the sign (𝄋)

D.S. al coda - return to the sign, proceed to the coda sign, then skip to the coda and finish the song

D.S. al fine - return to the sign and sing to the fine

fine - end

grazioso - gracefully

IPA- the International Phonetic Alphabet: a standard representation of the sounds of spoken language

Late Romantic/Impressionistic period of music - a movement in European classical music, mainly in France, that began in the late 19th century and continued into the middle of the 20th century

operetta - a genre of light opera: the precursor to Musical Theatre

primary triad - one of three triads, (tonic, subdominant, dominant) built from thirds

repetition - a compositional technique accomplished by repeating the same melodic patterns exactly

sequence - a compositional technique consisting of repeating the same melodic patterns at a different pitch

simile - to continue in the same manner

vivace - lively, quick, brisk tempo

Review: Lesson 9

1. Check the appropriate answer for each of the following questions.

a. A short aria is called an:

___cantata
___arietta

b. A compositional technique consisiting of repeating the same melodic patterns at a different pitch is called a:

___sequence
___repetition

c. The Italian word that means to continue in the same manner is:

___vivace
___simile

d. The Late Romantic/Impressionistic period of music began in which century?

___18th
___19th

e. The Italian word that means gracefully is:

___grazioso
___simile

f. This means return to the sign and sing to the *fine.*

___D.S. al coda
___D.S. al fine

g. This is the same as 2/2 time.

___common time
___alla breve/cut time

h. This means a lively, quick, brisk tempo.

___vivace
___arietta

i. This means return to the beginning.

___da capo (D.C.)
___D.C. al fine

j. This is one of three triads, (tonic, subdominant, dominant) built from thirds.

___primary triad
___coda

2. Complete the following crossword puzzle using the terms from this level.

Level 5 Crossword

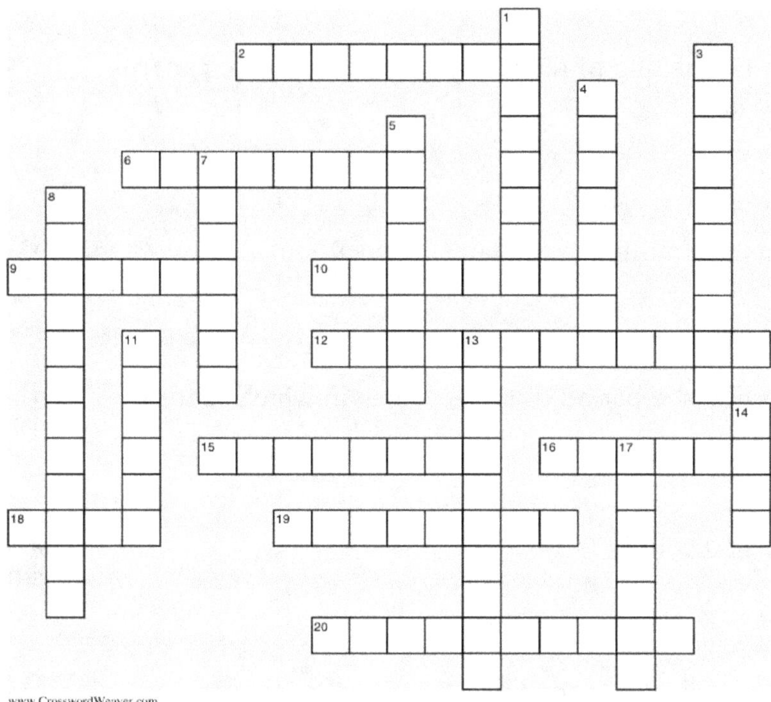

ACROSS

2 a genre of light opera. The precursor to Musical Theatre
6 return to the sign and sing to the fine (mutliple words)
9 to continue in the same manner
10 gracefully
12 Impressionistic period of music- a movement in European classical music, mainly in France, that began in the late 19th century and continued into the middle of the 20th century. (two words)
15 a compositional technique consisting of repeating the same melodic patterns at a different pitch.
16 return to the beginning (two words)
18 end
19 return to the beginning and sing to the fine (multiple words)
20 the same as 4 / 4 time (two words)

DOWN

1 return to the sign (two words)
3 a vocal form popular in the Baroque era, with an ABA form
4 return to the sign, proceed to the coda sign, then skip to the coda and finish the song (multiple words)
5 brilliant, lyric vocal style originating in Italy in the 18th & early 19th centuries (two words)
7 a short aria
8 one of three triads, (tonic, subdominant, dominant) built from thirds (two words)
11 lively, quick, brisk tempo
13 a compositional technique accomplished by repeating the same melodic patterns exactly
14 a separate section at the end of a song
17 alla breve, the same as 2 / 2 time (two words)

crossword created at:
www.CrosswordWeaver.com

Lesson 10: Spotlight on Composers

An important part of music education is learning about the history of music. Studying composers allows for understanding the music we sing and why it was written the way it was. In this level, you will learn about George Frederic Handel & Alessandro Scarlatti.

GEORGE FREDERIC HANDEL

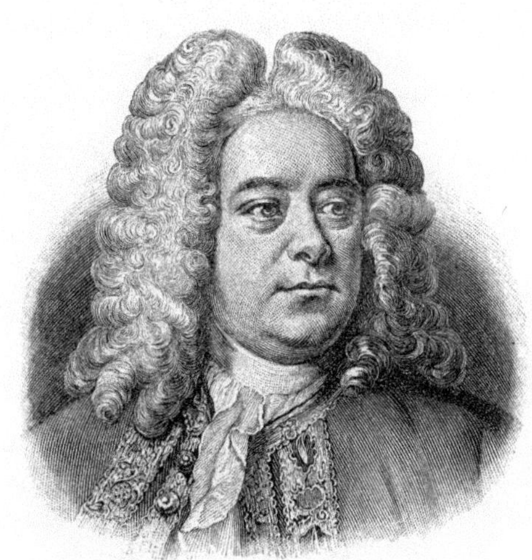

George Frederic Handel was born in the Baroque period of music on February 23rd, 1685 in Germany (the same year as Johann Sebastian Bach and Domenico Scarlatti). When Handel was young, his father did not want him to study music, but he was able to get a small clavichord, sneak it up to the top part of his house and practice when his family was asleep. Harpsichord and pipe organ were his favorite instruments.

Handel's father allowed the young Handel to take lessons after others noticed his talent. By the time he was 16 years old, he played for Frederick I of Prussia, Bononcini and Georg Phillipp Telemann. Handel attended law school briefly, but left after one year to become a full-time musician.

While in Italy, Handel wrote several vocal works including cantatas, oratorios and operas. In 1710, Handel traveled to London, England and decided to stay there. In 1717, his *Water Music,* an orchestral suite, was performed on the River Thames for King James and other Royalty. Between 1724-1725, Handel wrote three of his most famous operas, *Giulio Cesare, Tamerlano* and *Rodelinda.* Between 1711-1739, more than 25 of Handel's operas were premiered at The Queen's Theatre. (an opera house at which he was one of the managers) Handel also had success with his oratorios, especially his *Messiah* which premiered in 1742 with a chorus of 26 boys and five adult male soloists.This work still remains one of the most famous oratorios ever written and is still performed today.

Handel died on April 14th, 1759 at the age of 74. He was buried in Westminster Abbey. More than 3,000 people attended his funeral.

Best Known Vocal Works:
Oratorio: ***Messiah (The Hallelujah Chorus), Esther, Samson, Semele, Acis & Galatea & 26 others***
Opera: ***Giulio Cesare, Tamerlano, Rodelinda, Sosarme & 38 others***
He also wrote over 120 cantatas, numerous arias, trios and duets.

Other Significant Works:
Water Music as well as concertos, canticles, anthems, sonatas, hymns and church music.

ALESSANDRO SCARLATTI

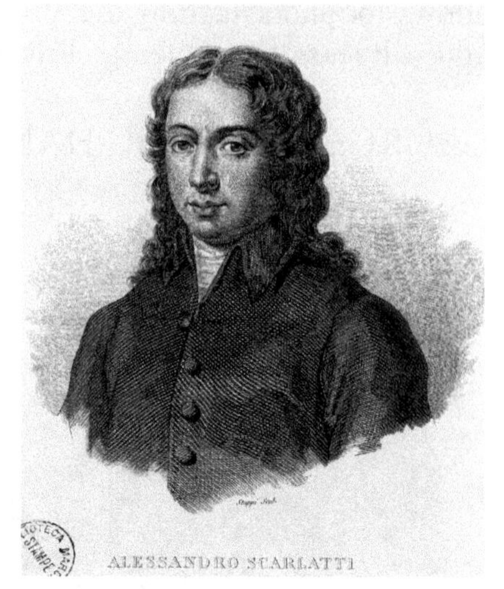

DEA/A. DAGLI ORTI/Contributor/Getty

Alessandro Scarlatti was born in the Baroque period of music on May 2, 1660 in Italy. When he was 12, he went to Rome to study with Carissimi. His successful opera *Gli Equivoci nell sembiante* was performed when he was only 19 years old. This opera caught the attention of Queen Christina of Sweden, and Scarlatti soon became her "Maestro di Cappella" (similar to a choir director).

In 1684, Scarlatti became the Maestro di Cappella to the viceroy of Naples. It was here he composed several operas and other vocal works. One of Scarlatti's famous patrons around 1702 was the renowned Medici family. He composed operas for this family in their private theaters.

Between 1717-1721, some of Scarlatti's most famous operas, *Telemaco, Marco Attilio Regolò,* and *La Griselda,* were performed at the Teatro Capranica in Rome. Scarlatti was considered to be the founder of the Neopolitan School of Opera. His music connected the Italian vocal styles of the Baroque period of music to the Italian vocal styles in the Classical period of music.

In addition to his operas and oratorios, Scarlatti also wrote more than 500 cantatas for solo voice. He also wrote masses and orchestral music as well. He died on October 24, 1725. His sons, Domenico Scarlatti and Pietro Filippo Scarlatti, are also well-known composers.

Best Known Vocal Works:

Operas: ***Gli equivoci nel sembiante, L'honestà negli amori, Il Pompeo, La Rosaura & Pirro e Demetrio***

Arias: **"Già il sole dal Gange," "O cessate di piagarmi," "Le Violette"**

Review: Lesson 10

1. Fill in the correct answer(s) to the following questions about George Frederic Handel & Alessandro Scarlatti.

George Frederic Handel

a. Handel was born in which country?________________________

b. What music period does he represent?______________________

c. Handel became highly skilled at two instruments at a young age. Name the instruments.___________________&_____________________

d. In what country did Handel live in for most of his life?______________________

e. Which of Handel's pieces was performed on the River Thames for King James and other Royalty?_______________________________

f. What is the name of Handel's most famous oratorio? _________________________

Alessandro Scarlatti

a. Scarlatti was born in which country?____________________

b. What music period does he represent?_____________________

c. How old was he when his first opera was performed?___________

d. It is said that Scarlatti founded the ______________________School of Opera.

e. When Scarlatti was 12, he moved to _______________to study music.

f. In 1689, which Queen hired Scarlatti as her "Maestro di Cappella?"

____

Level 5 Review Test

Answer the questions about the following musical example. (9 points)

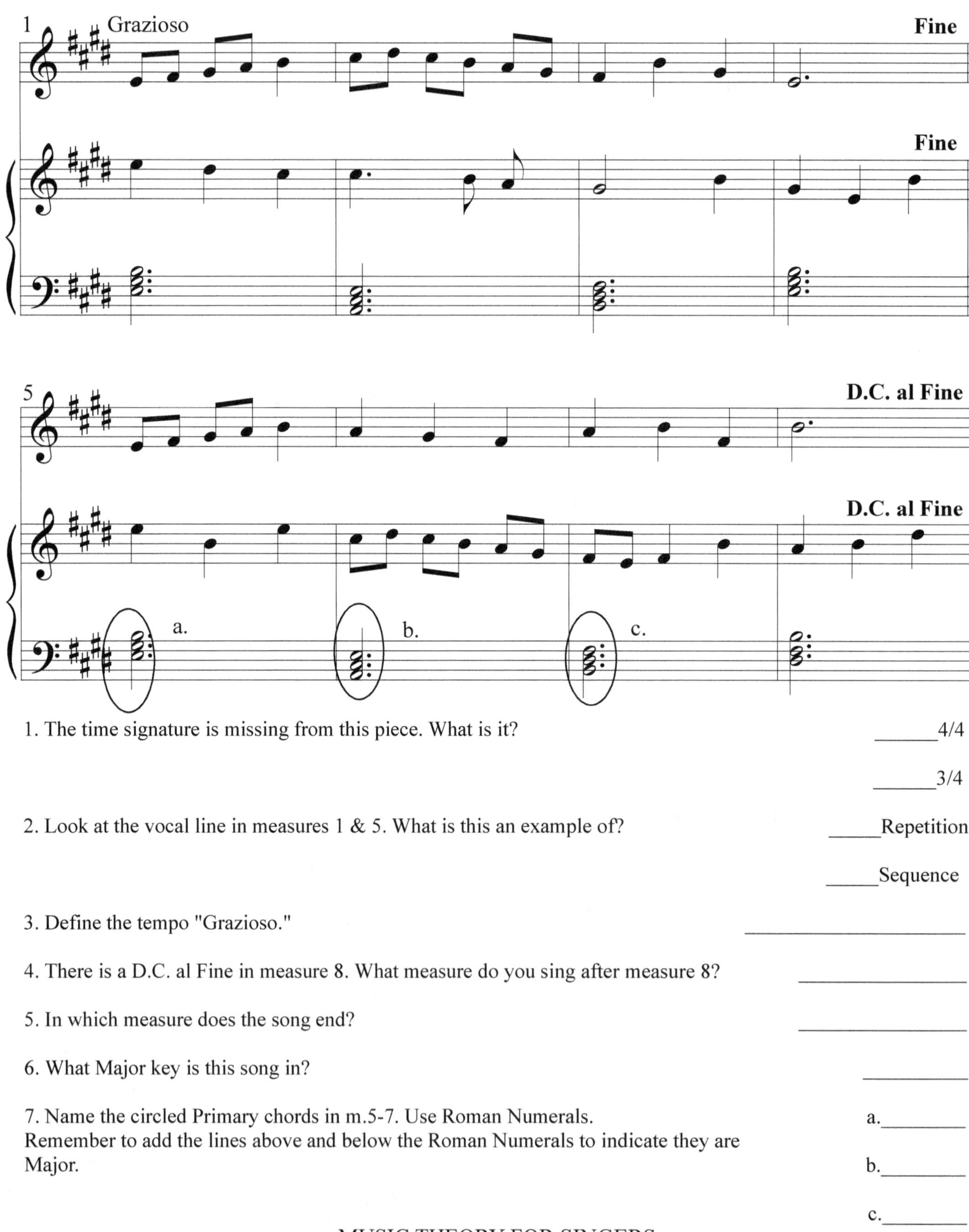

1. The time signature is missing from this piece. What is it? ______4/4

   ______3/4

2. Look at the vocal line in measures 1 & 5. What is this an example of? _____Repetition

   _____Sequence

3. Define the tempo "Grazioso." ______________________

4. There is a D.C. al Fine in measure 8. What measure do you sing after measure 8? ________________

5. In which measure does the song end? ________________

6. What Major key is this song in? __________

7. Name the circled Primary chords in m.5-7. Use Roman Numerals.
Remember to add the lines above and below the Roman Numerals to indicate they are Major.

   a.________

   b.________

   c.________

8. Name each note or rest and give it's value. For example: half note, 2 beats. (16 points-one for each note name, one for each value)

Note:____

Value:____

Note:____

Value:____

9. Add 3 bar lines and a double bar line to the following example. (4 points)

10. Add the missing time signature, then write the beats underneath the notes. (5 points-one for time signature, one for each correct measure)

11. Draw primary triads in both the treble and bass clef, then draw their corresponding Roman Numerals underneath. Pay attention to the key signature.
(12 points-one for each chord, one for each Roman Numeral)

Tonic Subdominant Dominant Tonic

12. Name the minor key signature then draw a triad with the minor Do (1) and a 3rd and 5th. (8 points)

Key of _____ minor Key of _____ minor Key of _____ minor Key of _____ minor

13. Name the following intervals. Indicate whether the interval is Major or minor using Maj. or min. For example, min.3rd. (20 points-one point each for name, one point each for type)

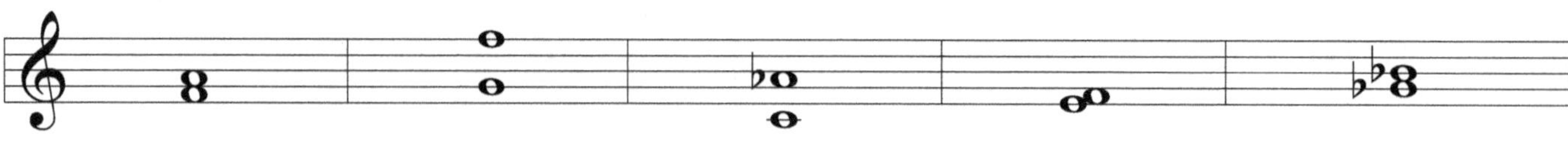

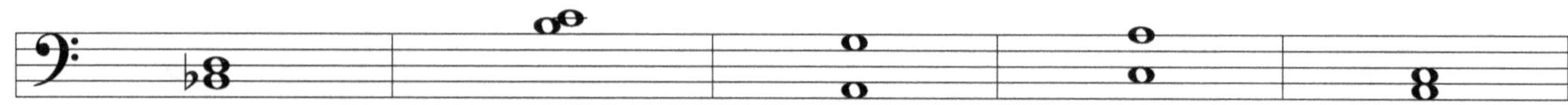

14. Draw a whole note above the given note to complete the requested harmonic interval. Pay attention to the key signatures, you may have to add an accidental. (8 points)

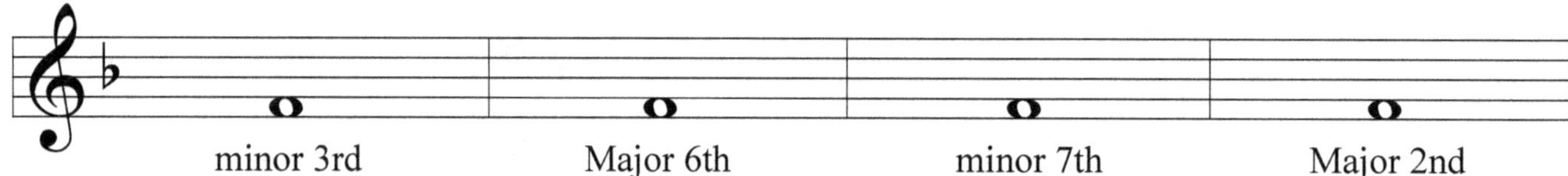

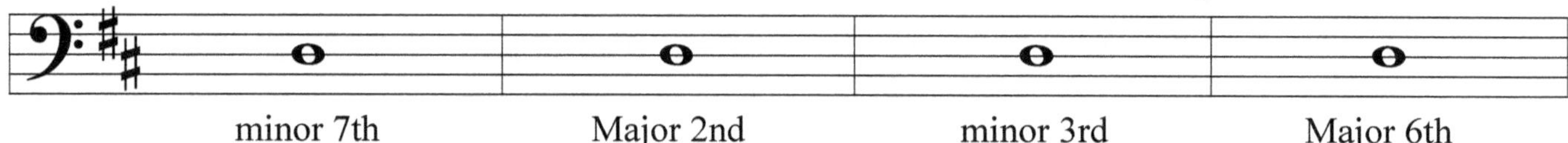

15. Each of these **minor** chords should have a Do (1), Mi (3), & Sol (5). Fill in the missing note for each chord in both clefs to create a root position triad. (8 points)

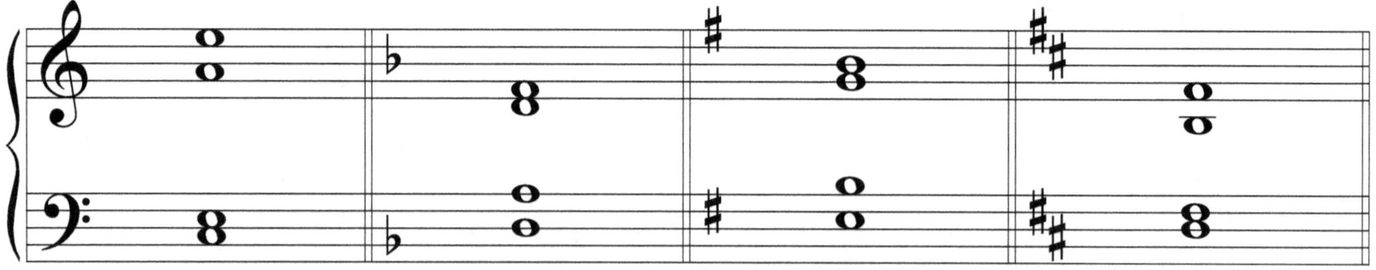

16. Write the note names and solfege under each note in the following examples. (3 points-1 point per correct measure: both solfege and notes must be correct)

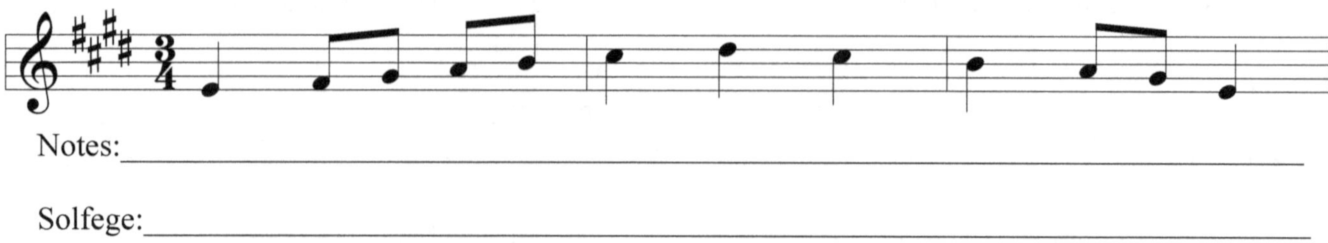

17. Check the English word that contains the same sound as the given IPA symbol. (4 points)

ɲ ___Canyon
___Nature

h ___Handy
___Extra

ð ___Cot
___Then

ŋ ___Ring
___Never

18. For the following questions, check the correct choice that best describes how the Spanish word would be pronounced. The IPA spelling is provided for you, in parentheses, after the word. (4 points)

baño (baɲo) ___bahn-yo
___bane-oh

rojo (roxo) ___row-ho
___row-jo

banco (baŋko) ___bank-oh
___bahn-koh

cansado (kanˈsaðo) ___con-sah-thoh
___can-say-doh

19. Fill in the correct answer using the musical terms in this level. (5 points)

a. ________________________is a brilliant, lyric vocal style from Italy in the 18th & 19th centuries.

b. ________________means to continue in the same manner.

c. _____________________is the same as 4/4 time.

d. _____________ means return to the sign and sing to the *fine.*

e. _____________means "end."

20. For the following questions, write "George Frederic Handel" or "Alessandro Scarlatti" as your answer. (5 points)

a. This composer had over 3,000 people at his funeral._______________________________

b. This composer wrote the "Hallelujah" chorus.___________________________________

c. This composer wrote the aria "Gia'il Sole dal Gange."______________________________

d. This composer was born in the same year as Johann Sebastian Bach.__________________

e. This composer was famous for his Italian operas, oratorios and cantatas.______________

Final Score:_____________/111

answer key begins on the next page

Level 5 Review Test: Answers

Answer the questions about the following musical example. (9 points)

1. The time signature is missing from this piece. What is it?

   ______4/4

   __X__3/4

2. Look at the vocal line in measures 1 & 5. What is this an example of?

   __X__Repetition

   _____Sequence

3. Define the tempo "Grazioso." gracefully

4. There is a D.C. al Fine in measure 8. What measure do you sing after measure 8? measure 1

5. In which measure does the song end? measure 4

6. What Major key is this song in? E Major

7. Name the circled Primary chords in m.5-7. Use Roman Numerals. Remember to add the lines above and below the Roman Numerals to indicate they are Major.

   a. I

   b. IV

   c. V

8. Name each note or rest and give it's value. For example: half note, 2 beats. (16 points-one for each note name, one for each value)

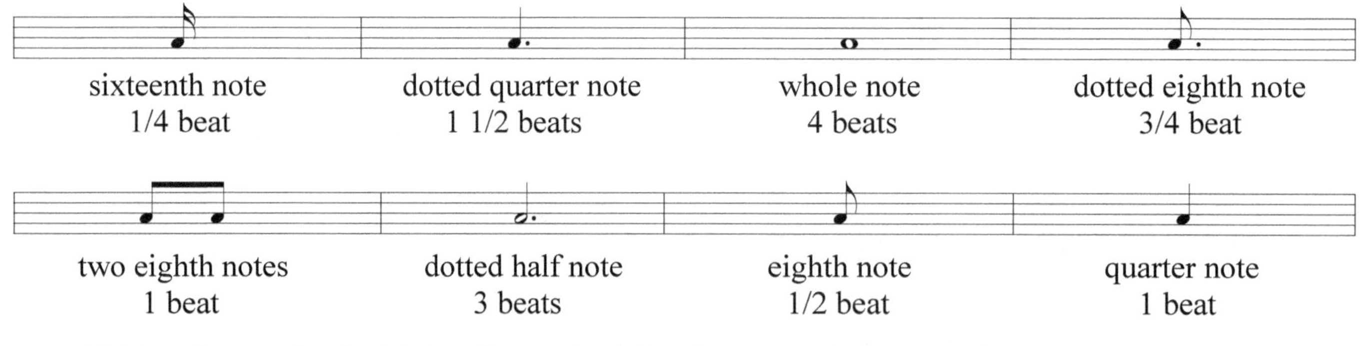

9. Add 3 bar lines and a double bar line to the following example. (4 points)

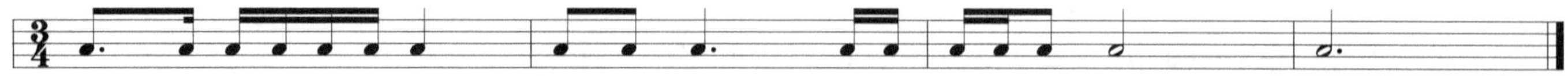

10. Add the missing time signature, then write the beats underneath the notes. (5 points-one for time signature, one for each correct measure)

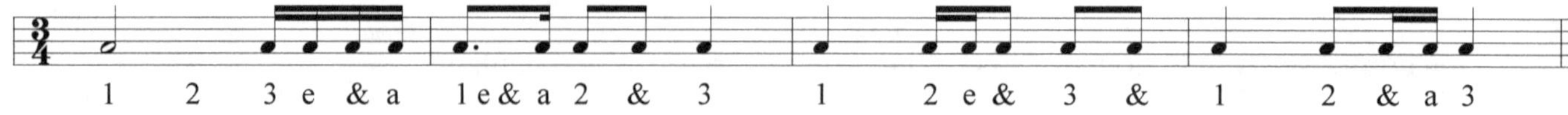

11. Draw primary triads in both the treble and bass clef, then draw their corresponding Roman Numerals underneath. Pay attention to the key signature. (12 points-one for each chord, one for each Roman Numeral)

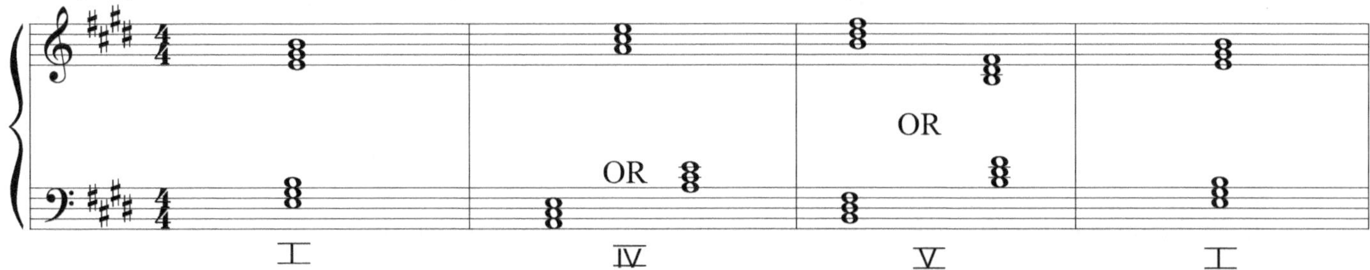

12. Name the minor key signature then draw a triad with the minor Do (1) and a 3rd and 5th. (8 points)

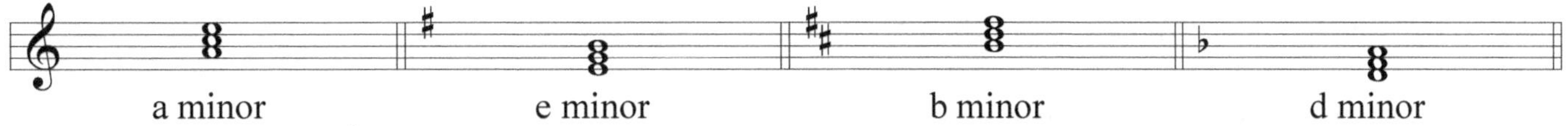

13. Name the following intervals. Indicate whether the interval is Major or minor using Maj. or min. For example, min.3rd. (20 points-one point each for name, one point each for type)

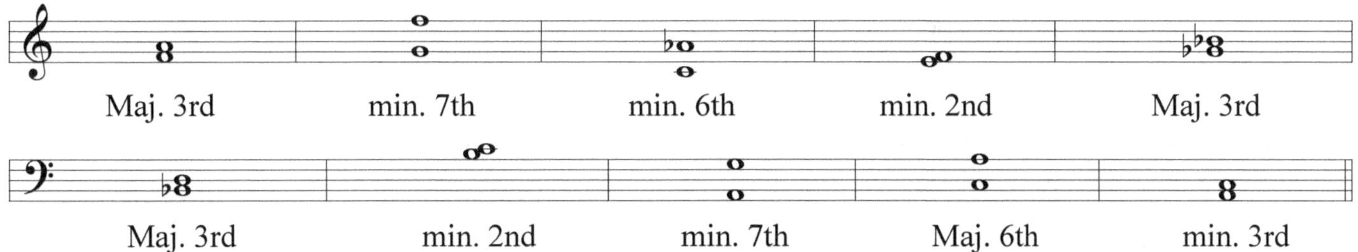

14. Draw a whole note above the given note to complete the requested harmonic interval. Pay attention to the key signatures, you may have to add an accidental. (8 points)

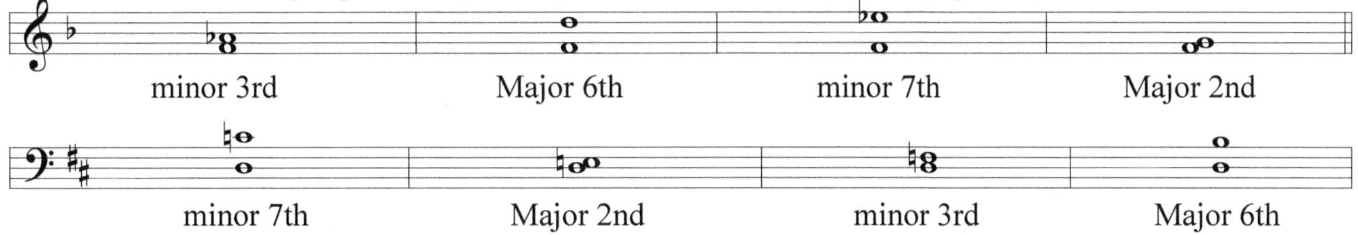

15. Each of these **minor** chords should have a Do (1), Mi (3), & Sol (5). Fill in the missing note for each chord in both clefs to create a root position triad. (8 points)

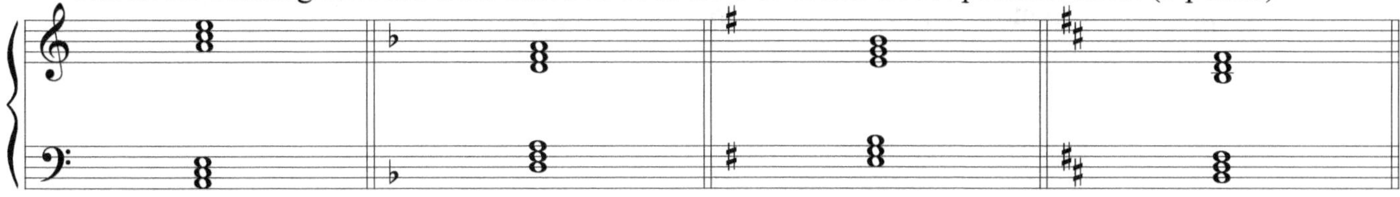

16. Write the note names and solfege under each note in the following examples. (3 points-1 point per correct measure: both solfege and notes must be correct)

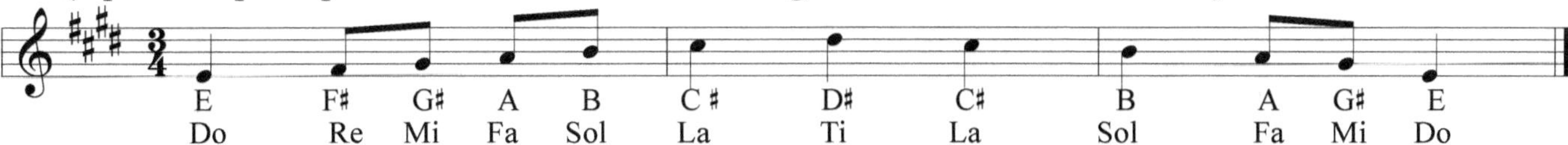

17. Check the English word that contains the same sound as the given IPA symbol. (4 points)

ɲ - Canyon h - Handy ð -Then ŋ- Ring

18. For the following questions, check the correct choice that best describes how the Spanish word would be pronounced. The IPA spelling is provided for you, in parentheses, after the word. (4 points)

baño (baɲo)- bahn-yo

rojo (roxo)- row-ho

banco (baŋko)- bahn-koh

cansado (kanˈsaðo)-con-sah-thoh

19. Fill in the correct answer using the musical terms in this level. (5 points)

a. bel canto is a brilliant, lyric vocal style from Italy in the 18th & 19th centuries.

b. simile means to continue in the same manner.

c. common time is the same as 4/4 time.

d. D.S. al fine means return to the sign and sing to the *fine*.

e. fine means "end."

20. For the following questions, write "George Frederic Handel" or "Alessandro Scarlatti" as your answer. (5 points)

a. This composer had over 3,000 people at his funeral. George Frederic Handel

b. This composer wrote the "Hallelujah" chorus. George Frederic Handel

c. This composer wrote the aria "Gia'il Sole dal Gange." Alessandro Scarlatti

d. This composer was born in the same year as Johann Sebastian Bach. George Frederic Handel

e. This composer was famous for his Italian operas, oratorios and cantatas. Alessandro Scarlatti

REFERENCES

Grout, Donald. *A History of Western Music.* New York, NY: W.W. Norton & Company, Inc., 1996.

Moriarty, John. *Diction*. Boston, MA: E. C. Schirmer Music Company, 1975.

Music Teachers' Association of California. *Certificate of Merit Voice Syllabus.* San Francisco: Music Teachers' Association of California, 2011.

Piston, Walter. *Harmony, Fifth Edition.* New York, NY: W.W. Norton & Company, Inc., 1987.

Plantinga, Leon. *Romantic Music, A History of Musical Style in Nineteenth-Century Europe.* New York, NY: W.W. Norton & Company, Inc., 1984.

Randel, Don Michael. *The Harvard Biographical Dictionary of Music.* Cambridge, Massachusetts: The Belknap Press of Harvard University Press, 1996.

Randel, Don Michael. *Harvard Concise Dictionary of Music.* Cambridge, Massachusetts: The Belknap Press of Harvard University Press, 1978.

Rushton, Julian. *Classical Music, A Concise History from Gluck to Beethoven.* London, England: Thames and Hudson Ltd., 1986.

The New Grove Dictionary of Music and Musicians. http://www.oxfordmusiconline.com., 2011

www.ingramcontent.com/pod-product-compliance
Lightning Source LLC
LaVergne TN
LVHW061256100826
845148LV00008B/1139

* 9 7 8 1 5 2 4 9 1 4 4 0 0 *